Elements in Quantitative Finance

edited by
Riccardo Rebonato
EDHEC Business School

CAUSAL FACTOR INVESTING

Can Factor Investing Become Scientific?

Marcos M. López de Prado
ADIA Lab

CAMBRIDGE
UNIVERSITY PRESS

Shaftesbury Road, Cambridge CB2 8EA, United Kingdom

One Liberty Plaza, 20th Floor, New York, NY 10006, USA

477 Williamstown Road, Port Melbourne, VIC 3207, Australia

314–321, 3rd Floor, Plot 3, Splendor Forum, Jasola District Centre, New Delhi – 110025, India

103 Penang Road, #05–06/07, Visioncrest Commercial, Singapore 238467

Cambridge University Press is part of Cambridge University Press & Assessment, a department of the University of Cambridge.

We share the University's mission to contribute to society through the pursuit of education, learning and research at the highest international levels of excellence.

www.cambridge.org
Information on this title: www.cambridge.org/9781009397292

DOI: 10.1017/9781009397315

First published 2023

A catalogue record for this publication is available from the British Library

ISBN 978-1-009-39729-2 Paperback
ISSN 2631-8571 (online)
ISSN 2631-8563 (print)

Causal Factor Investing

Can Factor Investing Become Scientific?

Elements in Quantitative Finance

DOI: 10.1017/9781009397315
First published online: October 2023

Marcos M. López de Prado
ADIA Lab
Author for correspondence: Marcos M. López de Prado,
marcos.lopezdeprado@adia.ae

Abstract: Virtually all journal articles in the factor investing literature make associational claims, in denial of the causal content of factor models. Authors do not identify the causal graph consistent with the observed phenomenon, they justify their chosen model specification in terms of correlations, and they do not propose experiments for falsifying causal mechanisms. Absent a causal theory, their findings are likely false, due to rampant backtest overfitting and incorrect specification choices. This Element differentiates between type-A and type-B spurious claims, and explains how both types prevent factor investing from advancing beyond its current phenomenological stage. It analyzes the current state of causal confusion in the factor investing literature, and proposes solutions with the potential to transform factor investing into a truly scientific discipline. This title is also available as Open Access on Cambridge Core.

Keywords: association, causation, causal inference, causal discovery, causal mechanism, confounder, factor investing, backtest overfitting

JEL Classification: G0, G1, G2, G15, G24, E44
AMS Classification: 91G10, 91G60, 91G70, 62C, 60E

ISBNs: 9781009397292 (PB), 9781009397315 (OC)
ISSNs: 2631-8571 (online), 2631-8563 (print)

Contents

1 Introduction

Science is more than a collection of observed associations. While the description and cataloging of phenomena play a role in scientific discovery, the ultimate goal of science is the amalgamation of theories that have survived rigorous falsification (Hassani et al. 2018). For a theory to be scientific, it is generally expected to declare the falsifiable causal mechanism responsible for the observed phenomenon (for one definition of falsifiability, see Popper 1963).[1] Put simply, a scientific theory explains *why* an observed phenomenon takes place, where that explanation is consistent with all the empirical evidence (ideally, including experimental results). Economists subscribe to this view that a genuine science must produce refutable implications, and that those implications must be tested through solid statistical techniques (Lazear 2000).

In the experimental sciences (physics, chemistry, biology, etc.), it is relatively straightforward to propose and falsify causal mechanisms through interventional studies (Fisher 1971). This is not generally the case in financial economics. Researchers cannot reproduce the financial conditions of the Flash Crash of May 6, 2010, remove some traders, and observe whether stock market prices still collapse. This has placed the field of financial economics at a disadvantage when compared with experimental sciences. A direct consequence of this limitation is that, for the past fifty years, most factor investing researchers have focused on publishing associational claims, without theorizing and subjecting to falsification the causal mechanisms responsible for the observed associations. In the absence of plausible falsifiable theories, researchers must acknowledge that they do not understand why the reported anomalies (risk premia) occur, and investors are entitled to dismiss their claims as spurious. The implication is that the factor investing literature remains in an immature, phenomenological stage.

From the above, one may reach the bleak conclusion that there is no hope for factor investing (or financial economics) to produce and build upon scientific theories. This is not necessarily the case. Financial economics is not the only field of study afflicted by barriers to experimentation (e.g., astronomers produce scientific theories despite the unfeasibility of interventional studies). Recent progress in causal inference has opened a path, however difficult, for advancing factor investing beyond its current phenomenological stage. The goal of this

---

[1] Strict falsificationism is not widely accepted among philosophers of science, and throughout this Element I do not follow Popper's falsificationist framework. I use the term "falsifiable" as the general requirement that theories must conform to the empirical evidence, without subscribing to a particular definition of what such conformity entails. *Mutatis mutandis*, this Element accommodates, and its results remain valid, under a number of competing accounts of what makes a theory "scientific."

Element is to help factor investing wake up from its associational slumber, and plant the seeds for the new field of "causal factor investing."

In order to achieve this goal, I must first recite the fundamental differences between association and causation (Section 2), and why the study of association alone does not lead to scientific knowledge (Section 3). In fields of research with barriers to experimentation, like investing, it has become possible to estimate causal effects from observational studies, through natural experiments and simulated interventions (Section 4). After laying out this foundation, I turn the reader's attention to the current state of causal confusion in econometrics (Section 5) and factor investing studies (Section 6). This state of confusion easily explains why factor investing remains in a phenomenological stage, and the proliferation of hundreds of spurious claims that Cochrane (2011) vividly described as the "factor zoo"[2] (Section 7). The good news is, once financial economists embrace the concepts described in this Element, I foresee the transformation of factor investing into a truly scientific discipline (Section 8).

This Element makes several contributions. First, I describe the logical inconsistency that afflicts the factor investing literature, whereby authors make associational claims in denial or ignorance of the causal content of their models. Second, I define the two different types of spurious claims in factor investing, type-A and type-B. These two types of spurious claims have different origins and consequences, hence it is important for factor researchers to distinguish between the two. In particular, type-B factor spuriosity is an important topic that has not been discussed in depth until now. Type-B spuriosity explains, among other literature findings, the time-varying nature of risk premia. Third, I apply this taxonomy to derive a hierarchy of empirical evidence used in financial research, based on the evidence's susceptibility to being spurious. Fourth, I design Monte Carlo experiments that illustrate the dire consequences of type-B spurious claims in factor investing. Fifth, I propose an alternative explanation for the main findings of the factor investing literature, which is consistent with type-B spuriosity. In particular, the time-varying nature of risk premia reported in canonical journal articles is a likely consequence of under-controlling. Sixth, I propose specific actions that academic authors can take to rebuild factor investing on the more solid scientific foundations of causal inference.

---

[2] A more appropriate name might have been "factor bestiary," because a zoo is populated only by real animals, while a medieval bestiary described in great detail real (e.g., lions, leopards, and elephants) as well as mythical animals (e.g. chimeras, griffins, and harpies), with equal conviction regarding the existence of both.

2 Association vs Causation

Every student of statistics, and by extension econometrics, learns that association does not imply causation. This statement, while superficially true, does not explain why association exists, and its relation to causation. Two discrete random variables X and Y are statistically independent if and only if $P[X = x, Y = y] = P[X = x]P[Y = y], \forall x, y$, where $P[.]$ is the probability of the event described inside the squared brackets. Conversely, two discrete random variables X and Y are said to be statistically associated (or codependent) when, for some (x, y), they satisfy that $P[X = x, Y = y] \neq P[X = x]P[Y = y]$. The conditional probability expression $P[Y = y|X = x] = P[X = x, Y = y]/P[X = x]$ represents the probability that $Y = y$ among the subset of the population where $X = x$. When two variables are associated, observing the value of one conveys information about the value of the other: $P[Y = y|X = x] \neq P[Y = y]$, or equivalently, $P[X = x|Y = y] \neq P[X = x]$. For example, monthly drownings (Y) and ice cream sales (X) are strongly associated, because the probability that y people drown in a month conditional on observing x ice cream sales in that same month does not equal the unconditional probability of y drownings in a month for some (x, y). However, the expression $P[Y = y|X = x] \neq P[Y = y]$ does *not* tell us whether ice cream sales cause drownings. Answering that question requires the introduction of a more nuanced concept than conditional probability: an intervention.

A data-generating process is a physical process responsible for generating the observed data, where the process is characterized by a system of structural equations. Within that system, a variable X is said to cause a variable Y when Y is a function of X. The structural equation by which X causes Y is called a causal mechanism. Unfortunately, the data-generating process responsible for observations is rarely known. Instead, researchers must rely on probabilities, estimated on a sample of observations, to deduce the causal structure of a system. Probabilistically, a variable X is said to cause a variable Y when *setting* the value of X to x increases the likelihood that Y will take the value y. Econometrics lacks the language to represent interventions, that is, setting the value of X (Chen and Pearl 2013). To avoid confusion between conditioning by $X = x$ and setting the value of $X = x$, Pearl (1995) introduced the do-operator, $do[X = x]$, which denotes the intervention that sets the value of X to x. With this new notation, causation can be formally defined as follows: $X = x$ causes $Y = y$ if and only if $P[Y = y|do[X = x]] > P[Y = y]$.[3]

---

[3] At first, it may seem counterintuitive that causality is defined in terms of a strict inequality (" >"), in contrast to the difference (" $\neq$ ") used to define association. The reason is, there is no need to consider the " < " case, due to complementary probabilities. For example, let $X = 1$ represent

For example, setting ice cream sales to x will not make y drownings more likely than its unconditional probability for any pair (x, y), hence ice cream sales are not a cause of drownings. In contrast, smoking tobacco is a cause of lung cancer, because the probability that y individuals develop lung cancer among a collective where the level of tobacco smoking is set to x (through an intervention) is greater than the unconditional probability of y individuals developing lung cancer, for some pair (x, y).[4]

Variables X and Y may be part of a more complex system, involving additional variables. The causal structure of a system can be represented through a directed acyclic graph, also denoted a causal graph.[5] While a causal graph does not fully characterize the data-generating process, it conveys topological information essential to estimate causal effects. Causal graphs declare the variables involved in a system, which variables influence each other, and the direction of causality (Pearl 2009, p. 12). Causal graphs help visualize do-operations as the action of removing all arrows pointing toward X in the causal graph, so that the full effect on Y can be attributed to setting $X = x$. This is the meaning of the *ceteris paribus* assumption, which is of critical importance to economists.

The causal graph in Figure 1 tells us that Z causes X, and Z causes Y. In the language of causal inference, Z is a confounder, because this variable introduces

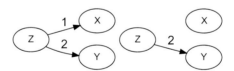

Figure 1 Causal graph of a confounder (Z), before (left) and after (right) a do-operation

receiving a vaccine against COVID-19, and $Y = 1$ represent developing COVID-19. For an effective vaccine, two causal statements are true. First, $P[Y = 1 | do[X = 1]] < P[Y = 1]$, which means that receiving the vaccine ($X = 1$) reduces the likelihood of developing the disease ($Y = 1$). Second, $P[Y = 0 | do[X = 1]] > P[Y = 0]$, which means that receiving the vaccine ($X = 1$) increases the likelihood of not developing the disease ($Y = 0$). One statement cannot be true without the other, and the redundancy is resolved by picking the latter.

[4] A variable X may be a necessary cause of Y, a sufficient cause of Y, a necessary-and-sufficient cause of Y, or neither a necessary-nor-sufficient cause of Y (also known as a contributory cause). I do not explain the difference in this Element because it is not required for the discussion that follows.

[5] Acyclic graphs have the advantage of allowing the factorization of the joint probability as a product of conditional probabilities between ancestors and descendants only. However, cyclic graphs may be preferred for representing bidirectional causality. Representing bidirectional causal relationships with acyclic graphs requires explicit temporal modeling and duplication of the graph over multiple time steps. Neither representation (cyclic or acyclic) is better, and it depends on the modeler's objectives. This Element focuses on the treatment of acyclic graphs, without dismissing the usefulness of cyclic graphical models.

an association between X and Y, even though there is no arrow between X and Y. For this reason, this type of association is denoted noncausal. Following with the previous example, weather (Z) influences ice cream sales (X) and the number of swimmers, hence drownings (Y). The intervention that sets ice cream sales removes arrow (1), because it gives full control of X to the researcher (X is no longer a function of Z), while keeping all other things equal (literally, *ceteris paribus*). And because X does not cause Y, setting $X = x$ (e.g., banning the sale of ice cream, $X = 0$) has no effect on the probability of $Y = y$. As shown later, noncausal association can occur for a variety of additional reasons that do not involve confounders.

Five conclusions can be derived from this exposition. First, causality is an extra-statistical (in the sense of beyond observational) concept, connected to mechanisms and interventions, and distinct from the concept of association. As a consequence, researchers cannot describe causal systems with the associational language of conditional probabilities. Failure to use the do-operator has led to confusion between associational and causal statements, in econometrics and elsewhere. Second, association does not imply causation, however causation does imply association because setting $X = x$ through an intervention is associated with the outcome $Y = y$.[6] Third, unlike association, causality is directional, as represented by the arrows of the causal graph. The statement "X causes Y" implies that $P[Y = y|do[X = x]] > P[Y = y]$, but not that $P[X = x|do[Y = y]] > P[X = x]$. Fourth, unlike association, causality is sequential. "X causes Y" implies that the value of X is set first, and only after that Y adapts. Fifth, the *ceteris paribus* assumption simulates an intervention (do-operation), whose implications can only be understood with knowledge of the causal graph. The causal graph shows what "other things" are kept equal by the intervention.

---

[6] Here I am referring to direct causes (a single link in the causal graph). There are causal structures where one cause may cancel another, resulting in *total* causation without association.

3 The Three Steps of Scientific Discovery

Knowing the causes of effects has long been a human aspiration. In 29 BC, ancient Roman poet Virgil wrote "happy the man, who, studying Nature's laws, / thro' known effects can trace the secret cause" (Dryden 1697, p. 71). It was not until around the year 1011 that Arab mathematician Hasan Ibn al-Haytham proposed a scientific method for deducing the causes of effects (Thiele 2005; Sabra 1989).

Science has been defined as the systematic organization of knowledge in the form of testable explanations of natural observations (Heilbron 2003). Mature scientific knowledge aims at identifying causal relations, and the mechanisms behind them, because causal relations are responsible for the regularities in observed data (Glymour et al. 2019).

The process of creating scientific knowledge can be organized around three critical steps: (1) the phenomenological step, where researchers observe a recurrent pattern of associated events, or an exception to such a pattern; (2) the theoretical step, where researchers propose a testable causal mechanism responsible for the observed pattern; and (3) the falsification step, where the research community designs experiments aimed at falsifying each component of the theorized causal mechanism.

3.1 The Phenomenological Step

In the phenomenological step, researchers observe associated events, without exploring the reason for that association. At this step, it suffices to discover that $P[X = x, Y = y] \neq P[X = x]P[Y = y]$. Further, a researcher may model the joint distribution $P[X = x, Y = y]$, derive conditional probabilities $P[Y = y|X = x]$, and make associational statements of the type $E[Y|X = x] = y$ (an associational prediction) with the help of machine learning tools. Exceptionally, a researcher may go as far as to produce empirical evidence of a causal effect, such as the result from an interventional study (e.g., Ohm's law of current, Newton's law of universal gravitation, or Coulomb's law of electrical forces), but without providing an explanation for the relationship. The main goal of the phenomenological step is to state "a problem situation," in the sense of describing the observed anomaly for which no scientific explanation exists (Popper 1994b, pp. 2–3). At this step, inference occurs by *logical induction*, because the problem situation rests on the conclusion that, for some unknown reason, the phenomenon will reoccur.[7]

---

[7] Reasoning by induction occurs when, given some premises, a probable conclusion is inferred non-reductively, by generalizing or extrapolating from specific cases to a general rule. The evidence to support this extrapolation may come from a large number of cases (enumerative induction) or a wide range of cases (variative induction). See Gensler (2010, pp. 80–117).

For instance, a researcher may observe that the bid-ask spread of stocks widens in the presence of imbalanced orderflow (i.e., when the amount of shares exchanged in trades initiated by buyers does not equal the amount of shares exchanged in trades initiated by sellers over a period of time), and that the widening of bid-ask spreads often precedes a rise in intraday volatility. This is a surprising phenomenon because under the efficient market hypothesis asset prices are expected to reflect all available information at all times, making predictions futile (Fama 1970). The existence of orderflow imbalance, the sequential nature of these events, and their predictability point to market inefficiencies, of unclear source. Such associational observations do not constitute a theory, and they do not explain why the phenomenon occurs.

3.2 The Theoretical Step

In the theoretical step, researchers advance a possible explanation for the observed associated events. This is an exercise in *logical abduction* (sometimes also called retroduction): Given the observed phenomenon, the most likely explanation is inferred by elimination among competing alternatives. Observations cannot be explained by a hypothesis more extraordinary than the observations themselves, and of various hypotheses the least extraordinary must be preferred (Wieten et al. 2020). At this step, a researcher states that X and Y are associated because X causes Y, in the sense that $P\big[Y = y | do[X = x]\big] > P[Y = y]$. For the explanation to be scientific, it must propose a causal mechanism that is falsifiable, that is, propose the system of structural equations along the causal path from X to Y, where the validity of each causal link and causal path can be tested empirically.[8] Physics Nobel Prize laureate Wolfgang Pauli famously remarked that there are three types of explanations: correct, wrong, and not even wrong (Peierls 1992). With "not even wrong," Pauli referred to explanations that appear to be scientific, but use unfalsifiable premises or reasoning, which can never be affirmed nor denied.

A scientist may propose a theory with the assistance of statistical tools (see Section 4.3.1), however data and statistical tools are not enough to produce a theory. The reason is, in the theoretical step the scientist injects extrastatistical information, in the form of a subjective framework of assumptions that give meaning to the observations. These assumptions are unavoidable, because the simple action of taking and interpreting measurements introduces subjective choices, making the process of discovery a creative endeavor.

---

[8] Following on the earlier examples, in the year 1900, Paul Drude was the first to offer a falsifiable explanation to Ohm's law of 1827; in the year 1915, Albert Einstein offered a falsifiable explanation for Newton's law of gravitation of 1687, and so on.

If theories could be deduced directly from observations, then there would be no need for experiments that test the validity of the assumptions.

Following on the previous example, the Probability of Informed Trading (PIN) theory explains liquidity provision as the result of a sequential strategic game between market makers and informed traders (Easley et al. 1996). In the absence of informed traders, the orderflow is balanced, because uninformed traders initiate buys and sells in roughly equal amounts, hence market impact is mute and the mid-price barely changes. When market makers provide liquidity to uninformed traders, they profit from the bid-ask spread (they buy at the bid price and sell at the ask price). However, the presence of informed traders imbalances the orderflow, creating market impact that changes the mid-price. When market makers provide liquidity to an informed trader, the mid-price changes before market makers are able to profit from the bid-ask spread, and they are eventually forced to realize a loss. As a protection against losses, market makers react to orderflow imbalance by charging a greater premium for selling the option to be adversely selected (that premium is the bid-ask spread). In the presence of persistent orderflow imbalance, realized losses accumulate, and market makers are forced to reduce their provision of liquidity, which results in greater volatility. Two features make the PIN theory scientific: First, it describes a precise mechanism that explains the causal link: orderflow imbalance → market impact → mid-price change → realized losses → bid-ask spread widening → reduced liquidity → greater volatility. Second, the mechanism involves measurable variables, with links that are individually testable. An unscientific explanation would not propose a mechanism, or it would propose a mechanism that is not testable.

Mathematicians use the term theory with a different meaning than scientists. A mathematical theory is an area of study derived from a set of axioms, such as number theory or group theory. Following Kant's epistemological definitions, mathematical theories are synthetic *a priori* logical statements, whereas scientific theories are synthetic *a posteriori* logical statements. This means that mathematical theories do not admit empirical evidence to the contrary, whereas scientific theories must open themselves to falsification.

3.3 The Falsification Step

In the falsification step, researchers not involved in the formulation of the theory independently: (i) deduce key implications from the theory, such that it is impossible for the theory to be true and the implications to be false; and (ii) design and execute experiments with the purpose of proving that the implications are false. Step (i) is an exercise in *logical deduction* because given some theorized premises, a falsifiable conclusion is reached reductively (Gensler 2010, pp. 104–110).

When properly done, performing step (i) demands substantial creativity and domain expertise, as it must balance the strength of the deduced implication with its testability (cost, measurement errors, reproducibility, etc.). Each experiment in step (ii) focuses on falsifying one particular link in the chain of events involved in the causal mechanism, applying the tools of mediation analysis. The conclusion that the theory is false follows the structure of a *modus tollens* syllogism (proof by contradiction): using standard sequent notation, if $A \Rightarrow B$, however $\neg B$ is observed, then $\neg A$, where A stands for "the theory is true" and B stands for a falsifiable key implication of the theory.

One strategy of falsification is to show that $P[Y = y | do[X = x]] = P[Y = y]$, in which case either the association is noncausal, or there is no association (i.e., the phenomenon originally observed in step (i) was a statistical fluke). A second strategy of falsification is to deduce a causal prediction from the proposed mechanism, and to show that $E[Y | do[X = x]] \neq y$. When that is the case, there may be a causal mechanism, however, it does not work as theorized (e.g., when the actual causal graph is more complex than the one proposed). A third strategy of falsification is to deduce from the theorized causal mechanism the existence of associations, and then apply machine learning techniques to show that those associations do not exist. Unlike the first two falsification strategies, the third one does not involve a do-operation.

Following on the previous example, a researcher may split a list of stocks randomly into two groups, send buy orders that set the level of orderflow imbalance for the first group, and measure the difference in bid-ask spread, liquidity, and volatility between the two groups (an interventional study, see Section 4.1).[9] In response to random spikes in orderflow imbalance, a researcher may find evidence of quote cancellation, quote size reduction, and resending quotes further away from the mid-price (a natural experiment, see Section 4.2).[10] If the experimental evidence is consistent with the proposed PIN theory, the research community concludes that the theory has (temporarily) survived falsification. Furthermore, in some cases a researcher might be able to inspect the data-generating process directly, in what I call a "field study." A researcher may approach profitable market makers and examine whether

---

[9] Sophisticated large asset managers routinely conduct so-called algo-wheel experiments to assess broker performance, however the results from these controlled experiments are rarely made public, and are generally unknown to the academic community (López de Prado 2017). See Webster and Westray (2022) for an example of a theoretical framework that covers this kind of execution experiments.

[10] Random spikes in orderflow imbalance allow researchers to observe the reaction of market makers while removing the influence of potential confounders. For the purpose of this experiment, a researcher is interested in orderflow imbalance fluctuations that market makers cannot rule out as random at their onset, however the researcher can determine to have been random (likely ex-post).

their liquidity provision algorithms are designed to widen the bid-ask spread at which they place quotes when they observe imbalanced order flow. The same researcher may approach less profitable market makers and examine whether their liquidity provision algorithms do not react to order flow imbalance. Service providers are willing to offer this level of disclosure to key clients and regulators. This field study may confirm that market makers who do not adjust their bid-ask spread in presence of orderflow imbalance succumb to Darwinian competition, leaving as survivors those whose behavior aligns with the PIN theory.

Popper gave special significance to falsification through "risky forecasts," that is, forecasts of outcomes y' under yet unobserved interventions x' (Vignero and Wenmackers 2021). Mathematically, this type of falsification is represented by the counterfactual expression $E[Y_{X=x'}|X = x, Y = y] \neq y'$, namely the expected value of Y in an alternative universe where X is set to x' (a do-operation) for the subset of observations where what actually happened is $X = x$ and $Y = y$.[11] Successful theories answer questions about previously observed events, as well as never-before observed events. To come up with risky forecasts, an experiment designer scrutinizes the theory, deducing its ultimate implications under hypothetical x', and then searches or waits for them. Because the theory was developed during the theoretical step without knowledge of (x', y'), this type of analysis constitutes an instance of out-of-sample assessment. For example, the PIN theory implied the possibility of failures in the provision of liquidity approximately fourteen years before the flash crash of 2010 took place. Traders who had implemented liquidity provision models based on the PIN theory (or better, its high-frequency embodiment, VPIN) were prepared for that black-swan and profited from that event (Easley et al. 2010, 2012, López de Prado 2018, pp. 281–300), at the expense of traders who relied on weaker microstructural theories.

3.4 Demarcation and Falsificationism in Statistics

Science is essential to human understanding in that it replaces unreliable inductive reasoning (such as "Y will follow X because that is the association observed in the past") with more reliable deductive reasoning (such as "Y will follow X because X causes Y through a tested mechanism M"). Parsimonious theories are preferable, because they are easier to falsify, as they involve controlling for fewer variables (Occam's razor). The most parsimonious surviving theory is not truer, however, it is better "fit" (in an evolutionary sense) to tackle more difficult problems posed by that theory. The most parsimonious

---

[11] For an introduction to counterfactuals, see Pearl et al. (2016, chapter 4).

surviving theory poses new problem situations, hence re-starting a new iteration of the three-step process, which will result in a better theory yet.

To appreciate the unique characteristics of the scientific method, it helps to contrast it with a dialectical predecessor. For centuries prior to the scientific revolution of the seventeenth century, academics used the Socratic method to eliminate logically inconsistent hypotheses. Like the scientific method, the Socratic method relies on three steps: (1) problem statement; (2) hypothesis formulation; and (3) *elenchus* (refutation), see Vlastos (1983, pp. 27–58). However, both methods differ in three important aspects. First, a Socratic problem statement is a *definiendum* ("what is X?"), not an observed empirical phenomenon ("X and Y are associated"). Second, a Socratic hypothesis is a *definiens* ("X is . . ."), not a falsifiable theory ("X causes Y through mechanism M"). Third, a Socratic refutation presents a counterexample that exposes implicit assumptions, where those assumptions contradict the original definition. In contrast, scientific falsification does not involve searching for contradictive implicit assumptions, since all assumptions were made explicit and coherent by a plausible causal mechanism. Instead, scientific falsification designs and executes an experiment aimed at debunking the theorized causal effect ("X does not cause Y"), or showing that the experiment's results contradict the hypothesized mechanism ("experimental results contradict M").[12]

The above explanation elucidates an important fact that is often ignored or misunderstood: not all academic debate is scientific, even in empirical or mathematical subjects. A claim does not become scientific by virtue of its use of complex mathematics, its reliance on measurements, or its submission to peer review.[13] Philosophers of science call the challenge of separating scientific claims from pseudoscientific claims the "demarcation problem." Popper, Kuhn, Lakatos, Musgrave, Thagard, Laudan, Lutz, and many other authors have proposed different demarcation principles. While there is no consensus on what constitutes a definitive demarcation principle across all disciplines, modern philosophers of science generally agree that, for a theory to be scientific, it must be falsifiable in some wide or narrow sense.[14]

---

[12] The reader should not conclude from these statements that the Socratic method has no place in science. The Socratic method can be helpful at certain steps of the scientific method, such as sharpening definitions (phenomenological step) and making all assumptions explicit (theoretical step).

[13] Some of the greatest scientists in history had limited mathematical training. The mathematical knowledge of Michael Faraday (1791–1867) did not reach beyond the simplest of algebra. What made Faraday one of the most influential scientists of all time was his ability to design experiments that elucidated causal mechanisms (Rao 2000, p. 281).

[14] This statement is hardly an endorsement of strict falsificationism *a la* Popper (1994b, pp. 82–86). It is merely an acknowledgement that scientists never cease to design experiments in an attempt to falsify a theory, if not with absolute certainty, at least with a sufficient degree of confidence.

The principle of falsification is deeply ingrained in statistics and econometrics (Dickson and Baird 2011). Frequentist statisticians routinely use Fisher's *p*-values and Neyman–Pearson's framework for falsifying a proposed hypothesis (H_0), following a hypothetico-deductive argument of the form (using standard sequent notation):

$$H_0 \Rightarrow P[data|H_0] \geq \alpha; P[data|H_0] < \alpha \vdash \neg H_0, \tag{1}$$

where *data* denotes the observation made and α denotes the targeted false positive rate (Perezgonzalez 2017). The above proposition is analogous to a *modus tollens* syllogism, with the caveat that H_0 is not rejected with certainty, as it would be the case in a mathematical proof. For this reason, this proposition is categorized as a stochastic proof by contradiction, where certainty is replaced by a preset confidence level (Imai 2013; Balsubramani and Ramdas 2016). Failure to reject H_0 does not validate H_0, but rather attests that there is not sufficient empirical evidence to cast significant doubt on the truth of H_0 (Reeves and Brewer 1980).[15] Accordingly, the logical structure of statistical hypothesis testing enforces a Popperian view of science in quantitative disciplines, whereby a hypothesis can never be accepted, but it can be rejected (i.e., falsified), see Wilkinson (2013). Popper's influence is also palpable in Bayesian statistics, see Gelman and Rohilla-Shalizi (2013).

Statistical falsification can be applied to different types of claims. For the purpose of this Element, it is helpful to differentiate between the statistical falsification of: (a) associational claims; and (b) causal claims. The statistical falsification of associational claims occurs during the phenomenological step of the scientific method (e.g., when a researcher finds that "X is correlated with Y"), and it can be done on the sole basis of observational evidence. The statistical falsification of causal claims may also occur at the phenomenological step of the scientific method (e.g., when a laboratory finds that "X causes Y" in the absence of any theory to explain why), or at the falsification step of the scientific method (involving a theory, of the form "X causes Y through a mechanism M"), but either way the statistical falsification of a causal claim always requires an experiment.[16] Most statisticians and econometricians are trained in the statistical falsification of

---

After over 100 years, physicists continue to test Einstein's theory of relativity in ingenious ways, and it is almost certain that one day they will succeed (for a recent falsification exercise, see Pogosian et al. 2022).

[15] In the words of Fisher (1971): "In relation to any experiment we may speak of this hypothesis as the *null hypothesis*, and it should be noted that the null hypothesis is never proved or established, but is possibly disproved, in the course of experimentation. Every experiment may be said to exist only in order to give the facts a chance of disproving the null hypothesis."

[16] As explained in Section 4.3, under certain assumptions the experiment used to falsify a causal claim may be simulated.

associational claims and have a limited understanding of the statistical falsification of causal claims in general, and the statistical falsification of causal theories in particular. The statistical falsification of causal claims requires the careful design of experiments, and the statistical falsification of causal theories requires testing the hypothesized causal mechanism, which in turn requires testing independent effects along the causal path. The next section delves into this important topic.

4 Causal Inference

The academic field of causal inference studies methods to determine the independent effect of a particular variable within a larger system. Assessing independent effects is far from trivial, as the fundamental problem of causal inference illustrates.

Consider two random variables (X, Y), where a researcher wishes to estimate the effect of X on Y. Let $E[Y|do[X = x_0]]$ denote the expected outcome of Y when X is set to x_0 (control), and let $E[Y|do[X = x_1]]$ denote the expected outcome of Y when X is set to x_1 (treatment). The average treatment effect (ATE) of X on Y is defined as

$$\text{ATE} = E[Y|do[X = x_1]] - E[Y|do[X = x_0]]. \tag{2}$$

In general, ATE is not equal to the observed difference, $E[Y|X = x_1] - E[Y|X = x_0]$. The observed difference between two states of X is

$$E[Y|X =x_1] - E[Y|X =x_0] = E[Y_{X=x_1}|X =x_1] - E[Y_{X=x_0}|X =x_0]$$
$$= \underbrace{E[Y_{X=x_1}|X =x_1] - E[Y_{X=x_0}|X =x_1]}_{\text{ATT}} + \underbrace{E[Y_{X=x_0}|X =x_1] - E[Y_{X=x_0}|X =x_0]}_{\text{SSB}},$$

$$\tag{3}$$

where $E[Y_{X=x_0}|X = x_1]$ is a counterfactual expression, representing the expected value of Y in an alternative universe where X is set to x_0, given that what actually happened is $X = x_1$. Naturally, $E[Y_{X=x_i}|X = x_i] = E[Y|X = x_i]$, for $i \in \{0, 1\}$, because the counterfactual expression (the left-hand side) replicates what actually happened (right-hand side).

The above equation splits the observed difference into two components, the so-called average treatment effect on the treated (ATT) and self-selection bias (SSB). The fundamental problem of causal inference is that computing ATT requires estimating the counterfactual $E[Y_{X=x_0}|X = x_1]$, which is not directly observable. What is directly observable is the difference $E[Y|X = x_1] - E[Y|X = x_0]$, however that estimand of ATT is biased by SSB. The impact of SSB on $E[Y|X = x_1] - E[Y|X = x_0]$ can be significant, to the point of misleading the researcher. Following the earlier example, suppose that Y is the number of drownings in a month, $X = x_0$ represents low ice cream monthly sales, and $X = x_1$ represents high ice cream monthly sales. The value of $E[Y|X = x_1] - E[Y|X = x_0]$ is high, because of the confounding effect of warm weather, which encourages both, ice cream sales and swimming. While high ice cream sales are associated with more drownings, it would be incorrect to infer that the former is a cause of the latter. The counterfactual

$E[Y_{X=x_0}|X = x_1]$ represents the expected number of drownings in a month of high ice cream sales, should ice cream sales have been suppressed. The value of that unobserved counterfactual is arguably close to the observed $E[Y_{X=x_1}|X = x_1]$, hence ATT ≈ 0, and the observed difference is largely due to SSB.

Studies designed to establish causality propose methods to nullify SSB. These studies can be largely grouped into three types: interventional studies, natural experiments, and simulated interventions.

4.1 Interventional Studies

In a controlled experiment, scientists assess causality by observing the effect on Y of changing the values of X while keeping constant all other variables in the system (a do-operation). Hasan Ibn al-Haytham (965–1040) conducted the first recorded controlled experiment in history, in which he designed a *camera obscura* to manipulate variables involved in vision. Through various ingenious experiments, Ibn al-Haytham showed that light travels in a straight line, and that light reflects from the observed objects to the observer's eyes, hence falsifying the extramission theories of light by Ptolemy, Galen, and Euclid (Toomer 1964). This example illustrates a strong prerequisite for conducting a controlled experiment: the researcher must have direct control of all the variables involved in the data-generating process. When that is the case, the *ceteris paribus* condition is satisfied, and the difference in Y can be attributed to the change in X.

When some of the variables in the data-generating process are not under direct experimental control (e.g., the weather in the drownings example), the *ceteris paribus* condition cannot be guaranteed. In that case, scientists may execute a randomized controlled trial (RCT), whereby members of a population (called units or subjects) are randomly assigned either to a treatment or to a control group. Such random assignment aims to create two groups that are as comparable as possible, so that any difference in outcomes can be attributed to the treatment. In an RCT, the researcher carries out the do-operation on two random samples of units, rather than on a particular unit, hence enabling a *ceteris paribus* comparison. The randomization also allows the researcher to quantify the experiment's uncertainty via Monte Carlo, by computing the standard deviation on ATEs from different subsamples. Scientists may keep secret from participants (single-blind) and researchers (double-blind) which units belong to each group, in order to further remove subject and experimenter biases. For additional information, see Hernán and Robins (2020) and Kohavi et al. (2020).

We can use the earlier characterization of the fundamental problem of causal inference to show how random assignment achieves its goal. Consider the situation where a researcher assigns units randomly to $X = x_0$ (control group) and $X = x_1$ (treatment group). Following with the earlier example, this is equivalent to tossing a coin at the beginning of every month, then setting $X = x_0$ (low ice cream sales) on heads and setting $X = x_1$ (high ice cream sales) on tails. Because the intervention on X was decided at random, units in the treatment group are expected to be undistinguishable from units in the control group, hence

$$E[Y_{X=x_0}|X = x_1] = E[Y_{X=x_0}|X = x_0] = E[Y_{X=x_0}] = E[Y|do[X = x_0]] \qquad (4)$$

$$E[Y_{X=x_1}|X = x_1] = E[Y_{X=x_1}|X = x_0] = E[Y_{X=x_1}] = E[Y|do[X = x_1]]. \qquad (5)$$

Random assignment makes $Y_{X=x_0}$ and $Y_{X=x_1}$ independent of the observed X. The implication from the first equation above is that SSB = 0. In the drownings example, $E[Y_{X=x_0}|X = x_1] = E[Y_{X=x_0}|X = x_0]$, because suppressing ice cream sales would have had the same expected outcome ($E[Y_{X=x_0}]$) on both, high sales months and low sales months, since the monthly sales were set at random to begin with (irrespective of the weather).

In conclusion, under random assignment, the observed difference matches both ATT and ATE:

$$
\begin{aligned}
& E[Y|X{=}x_1] - E[Y|X{=}x_0] \\
&= \underbrace{E[Y_{X=x_1}|X{=}x_1] - E[Y_{X=x_0}|X{=}x_1]}_{\text{ATT}} + \underbrace{E[Y_{X=x_0}|X{=}x_1] - E[Y_{X=x_0}|X{=}x_0]}_{\text{SSB}} \\
&= \underbrace{E[Y|do[X{=}x_1]] - E[Y|do[X{=}x_0]]}_{\text{ATE}} + \underbrace{E[Y|do[X{=}x_0]] - E[Y|do[X{=}x_0]]}_{\text{SSB}=0} \\
&= \text{ATE}.
\end{aligned}
\qquad (6)
$$

4.2 Natural Experiments

Sometimes interventional studies are not possible, because they are unfeasible, unethical, or prohibitively expensive. Under those circumstances, scientists may resort to natural experiments or simulated interventions. In a natural experiment (also known as a quasi-experiment), units are assigned to the treatment and control groups determined randomly by Nature or by other factors outside the influence of scientists (Dunning 2012). Although natural experiments are observational (as opposed to interventional, like controlled experiments and RCT) studies, the fact that the assignment of units to groups is assumed random enables the attribution of the difference in outcomes to the treatment. Put differently, Nature performs the do-operation, and the researcher's challenge is to identify the two random groups that enable a *ceteris paribus* comparison. Common examples of natural experiments include (1) regression discontinuity design (RDD); (2)

crossover studies (COSs); and (3) difference-in-differences (DID) studies. Case–control studies,[17] cohort studies,[18] and synthetic control studies[19] are not proper natural experiments because there is no random assignment of units to groups.

Regression discontinuity design studies compare the outcomes of: (a) units that received treatment because the value of an assignment variable fell barely above a threshold; and (b) units that escaped treatment because the value of an assignment variable fell barely below a threshold. The critical assumption behind RDD is that groups (a) and (b) are comparable in everything but the slight difference in the assignment variable, which can be attributed to noise, hence the difference in outcomes between (a) and (b) is the treatment effect. For further reading, see Imbens and Lemieux (2008).

A COS is a longitudinal study in which the exposure of units to a treatment is randomly removed for a time, and then returned. COS assumes that the effect of confounders does not change per unit over time. When that assumption holds, COSs have two advantages over standard longitudinal studies. First, in a COS the influence of confounding variables is reduced by each unit serving as its own control. Second, COS are statistically efficient, as they can identify causal effects in smaller samples than other studies. COS may not be appropriate when the order of treatments affects the outcome (order effects). Sufficiently long wash-out periods should be observed between treatments, to avoid that past treatments confound the estimated effects of new treatments (carryover effects). COS can also have an interventional counterpart, when the random assignment is under the control of the researcher. To learn more, see Jones and Kenward (2003).

When factors other than the treatment influence the outcome over time, researchers may apply a pre-post with-without comparison, called a DID study. In a DID study, researchers compare two differences: (i) the before-after difference

---

[17] In a case–control study, a researcher compares the incidence of a supposed causal attribute among two groups of units that differ in an outcome. For example, one group may be composed of individuals with lung cancer, and a second group by individuals without lung cancer. From the estimation of the odds ratio, the researcher may theorize (without proof) that smoking contributes to lung cancer.

[18] A cohort study is a longitudinal study where a researcher categorizes a cohort (a group of units who share a characteristic) into different subgroups based on their exposure to a particular factor, and then follows them over time to assess the incidence of the outcome of interest. Cohort studies can be retrospective (historical) or prospective (ongoing). Retrospective cohort studies are usually cheap and fast, however they are more vulnerable to publication bias and survivorship bias, among other problems.

[19] A synthetic control study is a longitudinal study where a researcher generates a synthetic control group. To do that, the researcher finds the linear combination of untreated units that is most similar to a treated unit before treatment, according to some common features. The treatment effect is computed as the difference between the observed outcome of the treated unit and the predicted outcome of the treatment on the synthetic control group. For a discussion, see Abadie (2021).

in outcomes of the treatment group; and (ii) the before-after difference in outcomes of the control group (where the random assignment of units to groups is done by Nature). By computing the difference between (i) and (ii), DID attempts to remove from the treatment effect (i) all time-varying factors captured by (ii). DID relies on the "equal-trends assumption," namely that no time-varying differences exist between treatment and control groups. The validity of the equal-trends assumption can be assessed in a number of ways. For example, researchers may compute changes in outcomes for the treatment and control groups repeatedly before the treatment is actually administered, so as to confirm that the outcome trends move in parallel. For additional information, see Angrist and Pischke (2008, pp. 227–243).

4.3 Simulated Interventions

The previous sections explained how interventional studies and natural experiments use randomization to achieve the *ceteris paribus* comparisons that result in SSB $= 0$. Each approach demanded stronger assumptions than the previous one, with the corresponding cost in terms of generality of the conclusions. For instance, the conclusions from a controlled experiment are more general than the conclusions from an RCT, because in the former researchers control the variables involved in the data-generating process in such a way that *ceteris paribus* comparisons are clearer. Likewise, the conclusions from an RCT are more general than the conclusions from a natural experiment, because in an RCT the researcher is in control of the random assignment, and the researcher performs the do-operation.

In recent decades, the field of causal inference has added one more tool to the scientific arsenal: when interventional studies and natural experiments are not possible, researchers may still conduct an observational study that *simulates* a do-operation, with the help of a hypothesized causal graph. The hypothesized causal graph encodes the information needed to remove from observations the SSB introduced by confounders, under the assumption that the causal graph is correct. The price to pay is, as one might have expected, accepting stronger assumptions that make the conclusions less general, but still useful.

Simulated interventions have two main applications: First, subject to a hypothesized causal graph, a simulated intervention allows researchers to estimate the strength of a causal effect from observational studies. Second, a simulated intervention may help falsify a hypothesized causal graph, when the strength of one of the effects posited by the graph is deemed statistically insignificant (once again, a *modus tollens* argument, see Section 3.4).

It is important to understand the difference between establishing a causal claim and falsifying a causal claim. Through interventional studies and natural experiments, subject to some assumptions, a researcher can establish or falsify a causal claim without knowledge of the causal graph. For this reason, they are the most powerful tools in causal inference. In simulated interventions, the causal graph *is* part of the assumptions, and one cannot prove what one is assuming. The most a simulated intervention can achieve is to disprove a hypothesized causal graph, by finding a contradiction between an effect claimed by a graph and the effect estimated with the help of that same graph. This power of simulated interventions to falsify causal claims can be very helpful in discovering through elimination the causal structure hidden in the data.

4.3.1 Causal Discovery

Causal discovery can be defined as the search for the structure of causal relationships, by analyzing the statistical properties of observational evidence (Spirtes et al. 2001). While observational evidence almost never suffices to fully characterize a causal graph, it often contains information helpful in reducing the number of possible structures of interdependence among variables. At the very least, the extra-statistical information assumed by the causal graph should be compatible with the observations. Over the past three decades, statisticians have developed numerous computational methods and algorithms for the discovery of causal relations, represented as directed acyclic graphs (see Glymour et al. 2019). These methods can be divided into the following classes: (a) constraint-based algorithms; (b) score-based algorithms; and (c) functional causal models (FCMs).

Constraint-based methods exploit conditional independence relationships in the data to recover the underlying causal structure. Two of the most widely used methods are the PC algorithm (named after its authors, Peter Spirtes and Clark Glymour), and the fast causal inference (FCI) algorithm (Spirtes et al. 2000). The PC algorithm assumes that there are no latent (unobservable) confounders, and under this assumption the discovered causal information is asymptotically correct. The FCI algorithm gives asymptotically correct results even in the presence of latent confounders.

Score-based methods can be used in the absence of latent confounders. These algorithms attempt to find the causal structure by optimizing a defined score function. An example of a score-based method is the greedy equivalence search (GES) algorithm. This heuristic algorithm searches over the space of Markov equivalence classes, that is, the set of causal structures satisfying the same conditional independences, evaluating the fitness of each structure based on a score calculated from the data (Chickering 2003). The GES algorithm is known to be consistent under certain assumptions, which means that as the sample size increases, the algorithm will converge to the true causal structure with probability approaching 1. However, this does not necessarily mean that the algorithm will converge to the true causal structure in finite time or with a reasonable sample size. GES is also known to be sensitive to the initial ordering of variables.

FCMs distinguish between different directed-acyclic graphs in the same equivalence class. This comes at the cost of making additional assumptions on the data distribution than conditional independence relations. A FCM models the effect variable Y as $Y = f(X, \varepsilon)$, where f is a function of the direct causes X and ε is noise that is independent of X. Subject to the aforementioned assumptions, the causal direction between X and Y is identifiable, because the independence condition between ε and X holds only for the true causal direction (Shimizu et al. 2006; Hoyer et al. 2009; and Zhang and Hyvaerinen 2009).

Causal graphs can also be derived from nonnumerical data. For example, Laudy et al. (2022) apply natural language processing techniques to news articles in which different authors express views of the form $X \rightarrow Y$. By aggregating those views, these researchers derive directed acyclic graphs that represent collective, forward-looking, point-in-time views of causal mechanisms.

Machine learning is a powerful tool for causal discovery. Various methods allow researchers to identify the important variables associated in a phenomenon, with minimal model specification assumptions. In doing so, these methods decouple the variable search from the specification search, in contrast with traditional statistical methods. Examples include mean-decrease accuracy, local surrogate models, and Shapley values (López de Prado 2020, pp. 3–4, López de Prado 2022a). Once the variables relevant to a phenomenon have been isolated, researchers can apply causal discovery methods to propose a causal structure (identify the links between variables, and the direction of the causal arrows).

4.3.2 Do-Calculus

Do-calculus is a complete axiomatic system that allows researchers to estimate do-operators by means of conditional probabilities, where the necessary and sufficient conditioning variables can be determined with the help of the causal graph (Shpitser and Pearl 2006). The following sections review some notions of do-calculus needed to understand this Element. I encourage the reader to learn more about these important concepts in Pearl (2009), Pearl et al. (2016), and Neal (2020).

4.3.2.1 Blocked Paths

In a graph with three variables $\{X, Y, Z\}$, a variable Z is a confounder with respect to X and Y when the causal relationships include a structure $X \leftarrow Z \rightarrow Y$. A variable Z is a collider with respect to X and Y when the causal relationships are reversed, that is, $X \rightarrow Z \leftarrow Y$. A variable Z is a mediator with respect to X and Y when the causal relationships include a structure $X \rightarrow Z \rightarrow Y$.[20]

A path is a sequence of arrows and nodes that connect two variables X and Y, regardless of the direction of causation. A directed path is a path where all arrows point in the same direction. In a directed path that starts in X and ends in Z, X is an ancestor of Z, and Z is a descendant of X. A path between X and Y is blocked if either: (1) the path traverses a collider, and the researcher has not conditioned on that collider or its descendants; or (2) the researcher conditions on a variable in the path between X and Y, where the conditioned variable is not a collider. Association flows along any paths between X and Y that are not blocked. Causal association flows along an unblocked directed path that starts in treatment X and ends in outcome Y, denoted the causal path. Association implies causation only if all noncausal paths are blocked. This is the deeper explanation of why association does not imply causation, and why causal independence does not imply statistical independence.

Two variables X and Y are d-separated by a (possibly empty) set of variables S if, upon conditioning on S, all paths between X and Y are blocked. The set S d-separates X and Y if and only if X and Y are conditionally independent given S. For a proof of this statement, see Koller and Friedman (2009, chapter 3). This important result, sometimes called the global Markov condition in Bayesian network theory,[21] allows researchers to assume that SSB $= 0$, and estimate ATE as

$$\begin{aligned} \text{ATE} &= E[Y|do[X = x_1]] - E[Y|do[X = x_0]] \\ &= E[E[Y|S, X = x_1] - E[Y|S, X = x_0]]. \end{aligned} \tag{7}$$

The catch is, deciding which variables belong in S requires knowledge of the causal graph that comprises all the paths between X and Y. Using the above concepts, it is possible to define various specific controls for confounding variables, including: (a) the backdoor adjustment; (b) the front-door adjustment; and (c) the method of instrumental variables (Pearl 2009). This is not a comprehensive list of adjustments, and I have selected these three adjustments in particular because I will refer to them in the sections ahead.

---

[20] These concepts are formally defined in Sections 7.1, 7.2, and 7.3.
[21] A Bayesian network is directed acyclic graph endowed with a set of conditional probability distributions. The conditional probability distributions specify the probability of each variable given its parent variables in the graph.

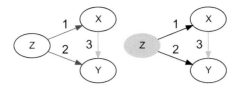

Figure 2 Example of a causal graph that satisfies the backdoor criterion, before (left) and after (right) conditioning on Z (shaded node)

4.3.2.2 Backdoor Adjustment

A backdoor path between X and Y is an unblocked noncausal path that connects those two variables. The term backdoor is inspired by the fact that this kind of paths have an arrow pointing into the treatment (X). For example, Figure 2 (left) contains a backdoor path (colored in red, $Y \leftarrow Z \rightarrow X$), and a causal path (colored in green, $Y \rightarrow X$). Backdoor paths can be blocked by conditioning on a set of variables S that satisfies the backdoor criterion. The backdoor criterion is useful when controlling for observable confounders.[22]

A set of variables S satisfies the backdoor criterion with regards to treatment X and outcome Y if the following two conditions are true: (i) conditioning on S blocks all backdoor paths between X and Y; and (ii) S does not contain any descendants of X. Then, S is a sufficient adjustment set, and the causal effect of X on Y can be estimated as:

$$P[Y = y | do[X = x]] = \sum_s P[Y = y | X = x, S = s] P[S = s]. \tag{8}$$

Intuitively, condition (i) blocks all noncausal paths, while condition (ii) keeps open all causal paths. In Figure 2, the only sufficient adjustment set S is $\{Z\}$. Set S is sufficient because conditioning on Z blocks that backdoor path $Y \leftarrow Z \rightarrow X$, and Z is not a descendant of X. The result is that the only remaining association is the one flowing through the causal path, thus adjusting the observations in a way that simulates a do-operation on X. In general, there can be multiple sufficient adjustment sets that satisfy the backdoor criterion for any given graph.

4.3.2.3 Front-Door Adjustment

Sometimes researchers may not be able to condition on a variable that satisfies the backdoor criterion, for instance when that variable is latent (unobservable). In that case, under certain conditions, the front-door criterion allows researchers to estimate the causal effect with the help of a mediator.

---

[22] I use here the nomenclature popularized by Pearl (2009); however, this form of adjustment was fully developed by Robins (1986) under the term g-formula.

A set of variables S satisfies the front-door criterion with regards to treatment X and outcome Y if the following three conditions are true: (i) all causal paths from X to Y go through S; (ii) there is no backdoor path between X and S; (iii) all backdoor paths between S and Y are blocked by conditioning on X. Then, S is a sufficient adjustment set, and the causal effect of X on Y can be estimated as:

$$P[Y = y|do[X = x]] = \sum_{s} P[S = s|X = x] \sum_{x'} P[Y = y|S = s, X = x']P[X = x'].$$

(9)

Intuitively, condition (i) ensures that S completely mediates the effect of X on Y, condition (ii) applies the backdoor criterion on $X \rightarrow S$, and condition (iii) applies the backdoor criterion on $S \rightarrow Y$.

Figure 3 provides an example of a causal graph with a latent variable Z (represented as a dashed oval) that confounds the effect of X on Y. There is a backdoor path between X and Y (colored in red, $Y \leftarrow Z \rightarrow X$), and a causal path (colored in green, $X \rightarrow M \rightarrow Y$). The first condition of the backdoor criterion is violated (it is not possible to condition on Z), however $S = \{M\}$ satisfies the front-door criterion, because M mediates the only causal path ($X \rightarrow M \rightarrow Y$), the path between X and M is blocked by collider Y ($M \rightarrow Y \leftarrow Z \rightarrow X$), and conditioning on X blocks the backdoor path between M and Y ($Y \leftarrow Z \rightarrow X \rightarrow M$). The adjustment accomplishes that the only remaining association is the one flowing through the causal path.

4.3.2.4 Instrumental Variables

The front-door adjustment controls for a latent confounder when a mediator exists. In the absence of a mediator, the instrumental variables method allows researchers to control for a latent confounder Z, as long as researchers can find a variable W that turns X into a collider, thus blocking the backdoor path through Z.

A variable W satisfies the instrumental variable criterion relative to treatment X and outcome Y if the following three conditions are true: (i) there is an arrow

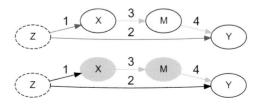

Figure 3 Example of a causal graph that satisfies the front-door criterion, before (top) and after (bottom) adjustment

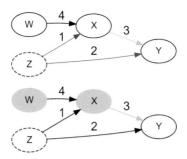

Figure 4 Example of a causal graph with an instrumental variable W, before (top) and after (bottom) adjustment

$W \to X$; (ii) the causal effect of W on Y is fully mediated by X; and (iii) there is no backdoor path between W and Y.

Intuitively, conditions (i) and (ii) ensure that W can be used as a proxy for X, whereas condition (iii) prevents the need for an additional backdoor adjustment to de-confound the effect of W on Y. Figure 4 provides an example of a causal graph with a latent variable Z that confounds the effect of X on Y. There is a backdoor path between X and Y (colored in red, $Y \leftarrow Z \to X$), and a causal path (colored in green, $X \to Y$). The first condition of the backdoor criterion is violated (it is not possible to condition on Z), and the first condition of the front-door criterion is violated (there is no mediator between X and Y). Variable W is an instrument, because there is an arrow $W \to X$ (arrow number 4), X mediates the only causal path from W to Y ($W \to X \to Y$), and there is no backdoor path between W and Y.

Assuming that Figure 4 represents a linear causal model, the coefficient $\frac{cov[X,Y]}{cov[X,X]}$ provides a biased estimate of the effect $X \to Y$, due to the confounding effect of Z. To estimate the unconfounded coefficient of effect $X \to Y$, the instrumental variables method estimates first the coefficient of the effect $W \to X \to Y$ as the slope of the regression line of Y on W, $r_{YW} = \frac{cov[Y,W]}{cov[W,W]}$, which is the product of coefficients of effects (3) and (4) in Figure 4. The coefficient of effect (4) can be estimated from the slope of the regression line of X on W, $r_{XW} = \frac{cov[W,X]}{cov[W,W]}$. Finally, the adjusted (unconfounded) coefficient of effect $X \to Y$ can be estimated as $\frac{r_{YW}}{r_{XW}}$. For further reading, see Hernán and Robins (2020, chapter 16).

5 Causality in Econometrics

Chen and Pearl (2013) reviewed six of the most popular textbooks in econometrics, concluding that they "deviate significantly from modern standards of causal analysis." Chen and Pearl find that most textbooks deny the causal content of econometric equations, and confuse causation with association. This section discusses several ways in which the econometrics literature often misunderstands causality.

5.1 Authors often Mistake Causality for Association

First, consider the joint distribution of (X, Y), and the standard econometric model, $Y_t = \beta_0 + \beta_1 X_t + \varepsilon_t$. Second, consider an alternative model with specification, $X_t = \gamma_0 + \gamma_1 Y_t + \zeta_t$. If regression parameters are characteristics of the joint distribution of (X, Y), it should be possible to recover one set of estimates from the other, namely $\hat{\gamma}_0 = -\hat{\beta}_0/\hat{\beta}_1$, $\hat{\gamma}_1 = 1/\hat{\beta}_1$, and $\hat{\zeta} = -\hat{\varepsilon}/\hat{\beta}_1$, because associational relations are nondirectional. However, least-squares estimators do not have this property. The parameter estimates from one specification are inconsistent with the parameter estimates from the alternative specification, hence a least-squares model cannot be "just" a statement on the joint distribution (X, Y). If a least-squares model does not model association, what does it model? The answer comes from the definition of the error term, which implies a directed flow of information. In the first specification, ε represents the portion of the outcome Y that cannot be attributed to X. This unexplained outcome is different from ζ, which is the portion of the outcome X that cannot be attributed to Y. A researcher that chooses the first specification has in mind a controlled experiment where X causes Y, and he estimates the effect coefficient β_1 under the least-squares assumption that $E[\varepsilon_t|X_t] = 0$, rather than $E[\varepsilon_t|Y_t] = 0$. A researcher that chooses the second specification has in mind a controlled experiment where Y causes X, and he estimates the effect coefficient γ_1 under the assumption that $E[\zeta_t|Y_t] = 0$, rather than $E[\zeta_t|X_t] = 0$. The vast majority of econometric models rely on least-squares estimators, hence implying *causal* relationships, not associational relationships (Imbens and Wooldridge 2009; Abadie and Cattaneo 2018).

By choosing a particular model specification and estimating its parameters through least-squares, econometricians inject extra-statistical information consistent with some causal graph. Alternatively, econometricians could have used a Deming (or orthogonal) regression, a type of errors-in-variables model that attributes errors to both X and Y. Figure 5 illustrates the regression lines of: (1) a least-squares model where X causes Y; (2) a least-squares model

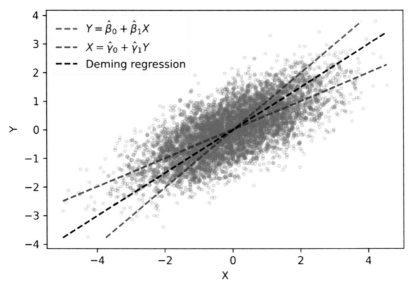

Figure 5 Three regression lines on the same dataset

where Y causes X; and (3) a Deming regression. Only result (3) characterizes the joint distribution (X, Y), without injecting extra-statistical information.

The realization that econometric equations model causal relationships may come as a surprise to many economics students and professionals. This surprise is understandable, because econometrics textbooks rarely mention causality, causal discovery, causal graphs, causal mechanisms, or causal inference. Economists are not trained in the estimation of Bayesian networks, design of experiments, or applications of do-calculus.[23] They are not taught that the causal graph determines the model's specification, not the other way around, hence the identification of a causal graph should always precede any choice of model specification. Instead, they have been taught debunked specification-searching procedures, such as the stepwise algorithm (an instance of selection bias under multiple testing, see Romano and Wolf 2005), the general-to-simple algorithm (see Greene 2012, pp. 178–182), or model selection through trial and error, see Chatfield (1995). Section 6.4.2.3 expands on this point, in the context of factor investing.

---

[23] Economists are often taught the method of instrumental variables, however econometrics textbooks motivate this method as a solution to the correlation between X and ε, once again comingling association with causation (see Chen and Pearl 2013, section 3.4). While instrumental variables can be helpful in some cases, they are a limited tool compared to the wide range of problems tackled by do-calculus.

5.2 Authors often Misunderstand the Meaning of β

The least-squares method estimates β in the equation $Y = X\beta + \varepsilon$ as[24]

$$\hat{\beta} = (X'X)^{-1}X'Y = (X'X)^{-1}X'(X\beta + \varepsilon) = \beta + (X'X)^{-1}X'\varepsilon. \tag{10}$$

For the estimate to be unbiased $(E[\hat{\beta}|X] = \beta)$, it must occur that $E[\varepsilon|X] = 0$. This is known as the exogeneity condition. There are two approaches for achieving exogeneity. The first approach, called implicit exogeneity, is to define the error term as $\varepsilon \equiv Y - E[Y|X]$, thus $E[\varepsilon|X] = E[Y - E[Y|X]|X] = E[Y|X] - E[Y|X] = 0$. Under this approach, $E[Y|X] = Y - \varepsilon = X\beta$, and β has merely a distributional (associational) interpretation, as the slope of a regression line. This is the approach adopted by most econometrics textbooks, see for example Greene (2012), Hill et al. (2011), Kennedy (2008), Ruud (2000), and Wooldridge (2009). A first flaw of this approach is that it cannot answer interventional questions, hence it is rarely useful for building theories. A second flaw is that it is inconsistent with the causal meaning of the least-squares model specification (Section 5.1).

The second approach, called explicit exogeneity, is to assume that ε represents all causes of Y that are uncorrelated to X. In this case, exogeneity is supported by a causal argument, not by an associational definition. When X has been randomly assigned, as in an RCT or a natural experiment, exogeneity is a consequence of experimental design. However, in purely observational studies, the validity of this assumption is contingent on the model being correctly specified. Under this second approach, $E[Y|do[X]] = X\beta$, and β has a causal interpretation, as the expected value of Y given an intervention that sets the value of X. More formally,

$$\beta = \frac{\partial E[Y|do[X]]}{\partial X}. \tag{11}$$

Defending the assumption of correct model specification requires the identification of a causal graph consistent with the observed sample. Absent this information, β loses its causal meaning, and reverts to the simpler associational interpretation that is inadequate for building theories and inconsistent with least-squares' causal meaning.

The *ceteris paribus* assumption, so popular among economists, is consistent with the causal interpretation of the estimated β, whereby the model simulates a controlled experiment. Haavelmo (1944) was among the first to argue that

---

[24] Throughout the Element, when a regression equation does not include an intercept, variable Y is assumed to have been centered.

most economists imply a causal meaning when they use their estimated β. Almost 80 years later, most econometrics textbooks continue to teach an associational meaning of the estimated β that contradicts economists' interpretation and use. Accordingly, economists are taught to estimate β as if it were an associational concept, without regard for causal discovery or do-calculus, while at the same time they interpret and use the estimated β as if it were a causal concept, leading to spurious claims.

5.3 Authors Often Mistake Association for Causality

Section 5.1 explained how economists often mean causation when they write about association. Oddly, economists also often mean association when they write about causation. A case in point is the so-called Granger causality. Consider two stationary random variables $\{X_t\}$ and $\{Y_t\}$. Granger (1969, 1980) proposed an econometric test for (linear) causality, based on the equation:

$$Y_t = \beta_0 + \sum_{i=1}^{I} \beta_i X_{t-i} + \sum_{j=1}^{J} \gamma_j Y_{t-j} + \varepsilon_t. \tag{12}$$

According to Granger, X causes Y if and only if at least one of the estimated coefficients in $\{\beta_i\}_{i=1,\ldots,I}$ is statistically significant. This approach was later expanded to multivariate systems, in the form of a vector autoregression specification, see Hamilton (1994, section 11.2).

   The term Granger causality is an unfortunate misnomer. The confusion stems from Granger's attempt to define causality in terms of sequential association (a characteristic of the joint distribution of probability), see Diebold (2007, pp. 230–231). However, sequentiality is a necessary, non-sufficient condition for causality (Section 2). Sequential association cannot establish causality, as the latter requires an interventional or natural experiment (Sections 4.1 and 4.2), and in the absence of these, a simulated intervention justified by a discovered or hypothesized causal graph (Section 4.3). For example, a Granger causality test will conclude that a rooster's crow (X_{t-1}) causes the sun to dawn (Y_t), because β_1 is statistically significant after controlling for lags of Y. And yet, it is trivial to falsify the claim that a rooster's crow is a cause of dawn, by silencing the rooster before dawn, or by forcing it to crow at midnight (an intervention). A second problem with Granger causality is that, if both X and Y are caused by Z (a confounder), Granger's test will still falsely conclude that X causes Y (see Figure 1). Granger causality is misleading in a causally insufficient multivariate time series (Peters et al. 2017, pp. 205–208). A third problem is that the test itself is susceptible to selection bias, because the selection of lagged variables involves multiple

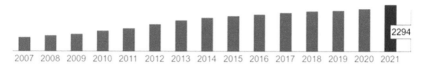

2294

2007 2008 2009 2010 2011 2012 2013 2014 2015 2016 2017 2018 2019 2020 2021

Figure 6 Citations of Granger (1969).

Source: Google Scholar, as of December 1, 2022[25]

testing across a large number of potential specifications that are not informed by a causal graph, for example through stepwise specification-searching algorithms. A fourth problem is that it assumes that the causal relation must be linear.

Granger (1969) remains one of the most-cited articles in the econometrics literature, with over 33,000 citations, and it has become Granger's second most-cited article. As Figure 6 illustrates, that publication receives thousands of new citations each year, and that number keeps rising, with 2,294 publications referencing it in the year 2021 alone. This confusion of association for causality has led to numerous misinformed claims in the factor investing literature (see Schuller et al. 2021 for a survey of claims based on Granger causality). While Granger causality may be used as a simple tool to help decide the direction of causal flow between two unconfounded variables (rather than the existence of causal flow), the field of causal discovery has developed more sophisticated methods to that purpose (see Peters et al. 2017, chapter 4).

I cannot end this section without recognizing a few remarkable economists who, defying the resistance from their peers, have fought to bring the rigor of causal inference into their field of study. Section 4.3.2.4 already discussed the method of instrumental variables, first proposed in 1928 by economist P. G. Wright. Section 5.2 mentioned Haavelmo's 1944 paper on the meaning of β, whose insights continue to be ignored today to a large extent (Pearl 2015). The original idea of the DID approach first appeared in labor economics, see Ashenfelter and Card (1986). In the year 2021, Joshua Angrist and Guido Imbens received (in conjunction with David Card) the Nobel Memorial Prize in Economics in recognition "for their methodological contributions to the analysis of causal relationships" in the context of natural experiments (see Section 4.2). Several authors have recently applied the RDD approach to corporate finance, such as Bronzoni and Iachini (2014), Flammer (2015), and Malenko and Shen (2016). Angrist and Pischke (2010) have called for a "credibility revolution," urging fellow economists to improve the reliability of their empirical work through the design of interventional studies and

---

[25] https://scholar.google.com/citations?hl=en&user=Q92731gAAAAJ

natural experiments. These academics offer a rare but inspiring example that ought to be emulated throughout the entire field of economics. On the other hand, asset pricing remains to this day staunchly oblivious to rigorous causal reasoning. Paraphrasing Leamer (1983), factor researchers have not yet taken the "con" out of *econ*ometrics, with the dire consequences described in the following section.

6 Causality in Factor Investing

The previous section outlined the prevailing state of confusion between association and causation in the field of econometrics. This section focuses on how financial economists have often (mis)applied econometrics to factor investing, leading to a discipline based on shaky foundations and plagued with false discoveries (Harvey 2017).

Factor investing can be defined as the investment approach that targets the exposure to measurable characteristics (called "factors") that presumably explain differences in the performance of a set of securities.[26] This is an evolution of the Asset Pricing Theory literature,[27] inspired by the seminal work of Schipper and Thompson (1981), that uses factor analysis and principal component analysis to validate those characteristics (Ferson 2019, p. 130). For example, proponents of the value factor believe that a portfolio composed of stocks with a high book-to-market equity (called "value stocks") will outperform a portfolio composed of stocks with a low book-to-market equity (called "growth stocks"). In search of supportive empirical evidence, factor researchers generally follow one of two procedures. In the first procedure, inspired by Fama and MacBeth (1973), a researcher gathers returns of securities (Y), explanatory factors (X), and control variables (Z). The researcher then estimates through least-squares the parameters (also called factor exposures or factor loadings) of a cross-sectional regression model with general form $Y = X\beta + Z\gamma + \varepsilon$ for each time period, and computes the mean and standard deviation of those parameter estimates across all periods (Cochrane 2005, pp. 245–251). In the second procedure, inspired by Fama and French (1993), a researcher ranks securities in an investment universe according to a characteristic, and carries out two parallel operations on that ranking: (a) partition the investment universe into subsets delimited by quantiles, and compute the time series of average returns for each subset; and (b) compute the returns time series of a long-short portfolio, where top-ranked securities receive a positive weight and bottom-ranked securities receive a negative weight. A researcher interested in a multifactor

---

[26] The term "factor investing" is another misnomer. The word "factor" has its origin in the Latin language, with the literal meaning of "doer" or "maker." Semantically, a factor is a cause responsible, in total or in part, for an effect. Ironically, the factor investing literature has not attempted to explain what does or makes the observed cross-section of expected returns.

[27] The field of Asset Pricing Theory uses the term "theory" in the mathematical sense, not in the scientific sense (see Section 3.2). For example, modern portfolio theory (MPT) derives results in risk diversification from the set of axioms proposed by Harry Markowitz's landmark 1952 paper. Modern portfolio theory results are true in a mathematical sense, by virtue of proven theorems, however they are not necessarily true in a physical sense. Modern portfolio theory was not derived through the process described in Section 3. Assessing the scientific validity of MPT's claims would require falsification of hypothesized causal mechanisms through testable implications (Section 3.3).

analysis will apply operations (a) and (b) once for each factor (for operation (a), this means further partitioning each subset). For each subset, the researcher then estimates through least-squares the parameters of a time-series regression model with general form $Y = X\beta + Z\gamma + \varepsilon$, where Y represents one time series computed in (a), X represents the (possibly several) time series computed in (b), and Z represents the times series of control variables chosen by the researcher.

The goal of both procedures is not to explain changes in average returns over time (a time-series analysis), but rather to explain differences in average returns across securities. The first procedure accomplishes this goal through averaging cross-sectional regressions coefficients computed on explanatory factors. The second procedure accomplishes this goal through a regression of quantile-averaged stock returns against the returns attributed to neutralized factors. Following the econometric canon, researchers state their case by showing that the estimated value of β is statistically significant, with the interpretation that investors holding securities with exposure to factor X are rewarded beyond the reward received from exposure to factors in Z.

6.1 Causal Content

Factor researchers almost never state explicitly the causal assumptions that they had in mind when they made various modeling decisions, and yet those assumptions shape their analysis. A different set of causal assumptions would have led to different data pre-processing, choice of variables, model specification, choice of estimator, choice of tested hypotheses, interpretation of results, portfolio design, etc. Some of these causal assumptions are suggested by the data, and some are entirely extra-statistical. I denote causal content the set of causal assumptions, whether declared or undeclared, that are embedded in a factor model's specification, estimation, interpretation, and use. Factor investing strategies reveal part of their causal content in at least four ways.

First, the causal structure assumed by the researcher determines the model specification. A factor investing strategy is built on the claim that exposure to a particular factor (X) causes positive average returns above the market's (Y), and that this causal effect $(X \rightarrow Y$, a single link in the causal graph) is strong enough to be independently monetizable through a portfolio exposed to X. A researcher only interested in modelling the joint distribution (X, Y) would surely use more powerful techniques from the machine learning toolbox than a least-squares estimator, such as nonparametric regression methods (e.g., random forest regression, support-vector regression, kernel regression, or regression splines). Factor researchers' choice of least-squares, explanatory variables, and conditioning variables, is consistent with the causal structure that they wish to impose (Section 5.1).[28]

Second, the estimation of β prioritizes causal interpretation over predictive power. If factor researchers prioritized predictive power, they would: (a) use estimators with lower mean-square error than least-squares, by accepting some bias in exchange for lower variance (Mullainathan and Spiess 2017; Athey and Imbens 2019). Examples of such estimators include ridge regression, LASSO, and elastic nets; or (b) use as loss function a measure of performance, such as the Sharpe ratio (for a recent example, see Cong et al. 2021). So not only researchers believe that Y is a function of X (a causal concept), but they are also willing to sacrifice as much predictive power (an associational concept) as necessary to remove all bias from $\hat{\beta}$. The implication is that factor researchers assume that the errors are exogenous causes of Y, uncorrelated to X (the explicit exogeneity assumption). Factor researchers' choice of least-squares is consistent with their interpretation of the estimated β as a causal effect (Section 5.2).

Third, factor researchers place strong emphasis on testing the null hypothesis of H_0: $\beta = 0$ (no causal effect) against the alternative H_1: $\beta \neq 0$ (causal effect), and expressing their findings through p-values. In contrast, machine-learners are rarely interested in estimating individual p-values, because they assess the importance of a variable in predictive (associational) terms, with the help of associational concepts such as mean-decrease accuracy (MDA), mean-decrease impurity (MDI), and Shapley values (López de Prado 2018). Factor researchers' use of p-values is consistent with the claim of a significant causal effect.[29]

Fourth, factor investors build portfolios that overweight stocks with a high exposure to X and underweight stocks with a low exposure to X, at the tune of one separate portfolio for each factor. A factor investor may combine those separate factor portfolios into an aggregate multifactor portfolio, however the reason behind that action is diversification, not monetizing a multifactor prediction. This approach to building portfolios stands in contrast with how other investors use predictions to form portfolios. Investors who rely on predictive models build portfolios exposed to the residual (ε) rather than portfolios exposed to a particular factor (X), hence for them biased estimates of β are not a concern. Factor researchers' approach to portfolio design is

---

[28] This is not to say that least-squares is the only approach to model causality. The point is that least-squares in particular implies that Y is a function of X (a particular direction of causation), unlike other types of regression methods, such as Deming regression.

[29] Such a causal claim is conditional on satisfying several assumptions, including that the model is correctly specified, and that p-values are adjusted for multiple testing. Section 6.4 explains why factor investing models typically do not satisfy these assumptions.

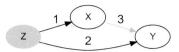

Figure 7 Causal graph for which the specification $Y = X\beta + Z\gamma + \varepsilon$ estimates the causal effect of X on Y, while adjusting for the confounding effect of Z

consistent with the monetization of a causal claim rather than a predictive (associational) claim.

In conclusion, the objective of a factor model such as $Y = X\beta + Z\gamma + \varepsilon$ is *not* to predict Y conditioned on X and Z ($E[Y|X, Z]$), but to estimate the causal effect of X on Y ($E[Y|do[X]]$), which can be simulated on the observed sample by controlling for confounder Z. The implication is that researchers use factors as if they had assumed explicit exogeneity, and their chosen model specification $Y = X\beta + Z\gamma + \varepsilon$ is consistent with a particular causal graph (see Section 5.2), of which Figure 7 is just one possibility among several. It is the responsibility of the researcher to declare and justify what particular causal graph informed the chosen specification, such that the exogeneity assumption holds true.

6.2 Omitted Mediation Analysis

Several papers have proposed alternative explanations for various factors, which can be grouped into two broad themes: (a) investment-based explanations; and (b) production-based explanations. For example, Fama and French (1996) argue that stocks approaching bankruptcy experience a price correction, which in turn is reflected as high value (a high book-to-market ratio). According to this explanation, investors holding portfolios of high-value stocks demand a premium for accepting a non-diversifiable risk of bankruptcy. Berk et al. (1999) argue that, should firms' assets and growth options change in predictable ways, that would impart predictability to changes in a firm's systematic risk and its expected return. Johnson (2002) explains that the momentum effect in stock returns does not necessarily imply investor irrationality, heterogeneous information, or market frictions, because simulated efficient markets for stocks exhibit price momentum when expected dividend growth rates vary over time. Gomes et al. (2003) simulate a dynamic general equilibrium economy, concluding that the size and value factors can be consistent with a single-factor conditional CAPM. Zhang (2005) simulates an economy that exhibits many empirical irregularities in the cross-section of returns. Sagi and Seasholes (2007) claim that backtested performance of momentum strategies is particularly good for firms with high revenue growth, low costs, or valuable growth options. Liu et al. (2009), Li et al. (2009), and Li and Zhang (2010) associate market anomalies with corporate investment levels, using Tobin's q-ratio (the ratio between a physical asset's market value and its replacement value). Liu and Zhang (2008) study the association between momentum portfolio returns and shifts in factor loadings on the growth rate of industrial production, concluding that the growth rate of industrial production is a priced risk factor. See Cochrane (2005, pp. 442–453) for additional explanations of factors, some of which are highly speculative or mutually contradictory.

These explanations, in the form of plausible economic rationales, do not rise to the level of scientific theories, for three primary reasons outlined in Sections 3 and 4. First, the authors of these explanations have not declared the causal relationship hypothetically responsible for the observed phenomenon. Second, the authors have not elucidated the ideal interventional study that would capture the causal effect of interest. A *Gedankenexperiment*, even if unfeasible, has the benefit of communicating clearly the essence of the causal relationship, and the counterfactual implications under various scenarios. Third, when the ideal interventional study is unfeasible, the authors have not proposed a method to estimate the causal effect through observational data (a natural experiment, or a simulated intervention). Consequently, while these economic rationales are plausible, they are also experimentally unfalsifiable. Following Pauli's criterion, the explanations proposed by factor investing researchers are "not even wrong" (Lipton 2016). As discussed in Section 3, scientific knowledge is built on falsifiable theories that describe the precise causal mechanism by which X causes Y. Value investors may truly receive a reward (Y) for accepting an undiversifiable risk of bankruptcy (X), but how precisely does this happen, and why is book-to-market the best proxy for bankruptcy risk? Despite of factor models' causal content, factor researchers rarely declare the causal mechanism by which X causes Y. Factor papers do not explain precisely how a firm's (or collection of firms') exposure to a factor triggers a sequence of events that ends up impacting stock average returns; nor do those papers derive a causal structure from the observed data; nor do those papers analyze the causal structure (forks, chains, immoralities); nor do those papers make an effort to explain the role played by the declared variables (treatment, confounder, mediator, collider, etc.); nor do those papers justify their chosen model specification in terms of the identified causal structure (an instance of concealed assumptions).

6.2.1 Example of Factor Causal Mechanism

For illustrative purposes only, and without a claim of accuracy, consider the following hypothetical situation. A researcher observes the tendency of prices (p_t) to converge toward the value implied by fundamentals (v_t). The researcher hypothesizes that large divergences between prices and fundamental values (HML) trigger the following mechanism: (1) As investors observe HML, they place bets that the divergence will narrow, which cause orderflow imbalance (OI); (2) the persistent OI causes permanent market impact, which over some time period (*h*) pushes prices toward fundamental values (PC, for price convergence).[30] An investment strategy could be proposed, whereby a fund manager acts upon (1) before (2) takes place.

As stocks rally, investors are more willing to buy them, making some of them more expensive relative to fundamentals, and as stocks sell off, investors are less willing to buy them, making some of them cheaper relative to fundamentals. The researcher realizes that the HML → OI → PC mechanism is disrupted by diverging price momentum (MOM), that is, the momentum that moves prices further away from fundamentals, thus contributing to further increases of HML. The researcher decides to add this information to the causal mechanism as follows: (3) high MOM affects future prices in a way that delays PC; and (4) aware of that delay, investors are wary of acting upon HML in the presence of high MOM (i.e., placing a price-convergence bet too early). Accordingly, MOM is a likely confounder, and the researcher must block that backdoor path HML ← MOM → PC. Fortunately, MOM is observable, thus eligible for backdoor adjustment (Section 4.3.2.2). But even if MOM were not observable, a frontdoor adjustment would be possible, thanks to the mediator OI (Section 4.3.2.3).

The above description is consistent with the following system of structural equations:

$$\mathrm{OI}_t := f_1 \underbrace{[p_t - v_t]}_{\mathrm{HML}_t} + \varepsilon_{1,t} \tag{13}$$

$$\underbrace{p_{t+h} - v_t}_{PC_{t+h}} := f_2[\mathrm{OI}_t] + f_3[\mathrm{MOM}_t] + \varepsilon_{2,t+h} \tag{14}$$

$$\mathrm{HML}_t := f_4[\mathrm{MOM}_t] + \varepsilon_{3,t} \tag{15}$$

where $\{f_i[.]\}_{i=1,2,3,4}$ are the functions associated with each causal effect (the arrows in a causal graph), and $\{\varepsilon_{i..}\}_{i=1,2,3}$ are exogenous unspecified causes. The symbol ":=" indicates that the relationship is causal rather than associational, thus asymmetric (e.g., the right-hand side influences the left-hand side, and not the other way around). The researcher applies causal discovery tools on a representative dataset, and finds that the derived causal structure is compatible

---

[30] I use the acronyms HML and MOM, common in the literature, without loss of generality. Fama and French (1993) and Carhart (1997) proposed some of the best-known definitions of value and momentum, however, this causal theory is congruent with alternative definitions.

with his theorized data-generating process. Using the discovered causal graph, he estimates the effect of HML on OI, and the effect of OI on PC, with a backdoor adjustment for MOM. The empirical analysis suggests that HML causes PC, and that the effect is mediated by OI. Encouraged by these results, the researcher submits an article to a prestigious academic journal.

Upon review of the researcher's journal submission, a referee asks why the model does not control for bid-ask spread (BAS) and market liquidity factors (LIQ). The referee argues that OI is not directly observable, and its estimation may be biased by passive traders. For instance, a large fund may decide to place passive orders at the bid for weeks, rather than lift the offers, in order to conceal their buying intentions. Those trades will be labeled as sale-initiated by the exchange, even though the persistent OI comes from the passive buyer (a problem discussed in Easley et al. 2016). The referee argues that BAS is more directly observable, and perhaps a better proxy for the presence of informed traders. The researcher counter-argues that he agrees that (5) OI causes market makers to widen BAS, however (6) PC also forces market makers to realize losses, as prices trend, and market makers' reaction to those losses is also the widening of BAS. Two consequences of BAS widening are (7) lower liquidity provision and (8) greater volatility. Accordingly, BAS is a collider, and controlling for it would open the noncausal path of association HML ← OI → BAS ← PC (see Section 6.4.2.2). While the referee is not convinced with the relevance of (6), he is satisfied that the researcher has clearly stated his assumptions through a causal graph. Readers may disagree with the stated assumptions, which the causal graph makes explicit, however, under the proposed causal graph everyone agrees that controlling for either BAS or LIQ or VOL would be a mistake.

The final causal path and causal graph are reflected in Figure 8. By providing this causal graph and mechanism, the researcher has opened himself to falsification. Referees and readers may propose experiments designed to challenge every link in the causal graph. For example, researchers can test link (1) through a natural experiment, by taking advantage that fundamental data is updated at random time differences between stocks. The treatment effect for link (1) may be estimated as the difference in OI over a given period between stocks where HML has been updated versus stocks where HML has not been updated yet. Links (2), (5), (6), (7), and (8) may be tested through controlled and natural experiments similar to those mentioned in Section 3.3. Link (3) is a mathematical statement that requires no empirical testing. To test link (4), a researcher may split stocks with similar HML into two groups (a cohort study, see Section 4.2): the first group is composed of stocks where MOM is increasing HML, and the second group is composed of stocks where MOM is reducing

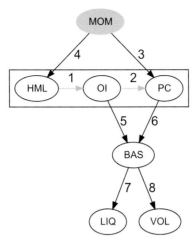

Figure 8 Example of a hypothesized causal mechanism of HML (in the box) within a hypothesized causal graph

HML. Since the split is not random, the researcher must verify that the two groups are comparable in all respects other than MOM's direction. The treatment effect may be measured as the two groups' difference in: (a) sentiment extracted from text, such as analyst reports, financial news, social media (see Das and Chen 2007; Baker and Wurgler 2007); (b) sentiment from surveys; or (c) exposures reports in SEC 13F forms. If link (4) is true, MOM dampens investors' appetite for HML's contrarian bets, which is reflected in the groups' difference.

These experiments are by no means unique, and many alternatives exist. The opportunities for debunking this theory will only grow as more alternative datasets become available. Contrast this openness with the narrow opportunities offered by factor investing articles currently published in journals, which are essentially limited to: (a) in-sample replication of a backtest, and (b) structural break analyses for in-sample versus out-of-sample performance.

6.3 Causal Denial

Associational investment strategies do not have causal content. Examples include statistical arbitrage (Rad et al. 2016), sentiment analysis (Katayama and Tsuda 2020), or alpha capture (Isichenko 2021, pp. 129–154). Authors of associational investment strategies state their claims in terms of distributional properties, for example, stationarity, ergodicity, normality, homoscedasticity, serial independence, and linearity. The presence of causal content sets factor investing strategies apart, because these investment strategies make causal claims. A causal claim implies knowledge of the data-generating process responsible, among other attributes, for all distributional properties claimed by associational studies. Causal claims therefore require stronger empirical evidence and level of disclosure than mere associational claims. In the context of investment strategies, this translates among other disclosures into: (i) making all causal assumptions explicit through a causal graph; (ii) stating the falsifiable causal mechanism responsible for a claimed causal effect; and (iii) providing empirical evidence in support of (i) and (ii).

Should factor researchers declare causal graphs and causal mechanisms, they would enjoy two benefits essential to scientific discovery. First, causal graphs like the one displayed in Figure 8 would allow researchers to make their causal assumptions explicit, communicate clearly the role played by each variable in the hypothesized phenomenon, and apply do-calculus rules for debiasing estimates. This information is indispensable for justifying the proposed model specification. Second, stating the causal mechanism would provide an opportunity for falsifying a factor theory without resorting to backtests. Even if a researcher p-hacked the factor model, the research community would still be able to design creative experiments aimed at testing independently the implications of every link in the theorized causal path, employing alternative datasets. Peer-reviewers' work would not be reduced to mechanical attempts at reproducing the author's calculations.

The omission of causal graphs and causal mechanisms highlights the logical inconsistency at the heart of the factor investing literature: on one hand, researchers inject causal content into their models, and use those models in a way consistent with a causal interpretation (Section 6.1). On the other hand, researchers almost never state a causal graph or falsifiable causal mechanism, in denial or ignorance of the causal content of factor models, hence depriving the scientific community of the opportunity to design experiments that challenge the underlying theory and assumptions (Section 6.2). Under the current state of causal confusion, researchers report the estimated β devoid of its causal meaning (the effect on Y of an intervention on X), and present p-values as if they merely conveyed the strength of associations of unknown origin (causal and noncausal combined).

The practical implication of this logical inconsistency is that the factor investing literature remains at a phenomenological stage, where spurious claims of investment factors are accepted without challenge. Put simply: without a causal mechanism, there is no investment theory; without investment theory, there is no falsification; without falsification, investing cannot be scientific.

This does not mean that investment factors do not exist; however, it means that the empirical evidence presented by factor researchers is insufficient and flawed by scientific standards. Causal denial (or ignorance) is a likely reason for the proliferation of spurious claims in the factor investing studies, and the poor performance delivered by the factor-based investment funds, for the reasons explained next.

6.4 Spurious Investment Factors

The out-of-sample performance of factor investing has been disappointing. One of the broadest factor investing indices is the Bloomberg–Goldman Sachs Asset Management US Equity Multi-Factor Index (BBG code: BGSUSEMF <Index>). It tracks the long/short performance of the momentum, value, quality, and low-risk factors in US stocks (Bloomberg 2021). Its annualized Sharpe ratio from May 2, 2007 (the inception date) to December 2, 2022 (this Element's submission date) has been 0.29 (t-stat = 1.16, p-value = 0.12), and the average annualized return has been 1.13 percent. This performance does not include: (a) transaction costs; (b) market impact of order execution; (c) cost of borrowing stocks for shorting positions; (d) management and incentive fees. Also, this performance assigns a favorable 0 percent risk-free rate when computing the excess returns. Using the 6-month US Government bond rates (BBG code: USGG6M <Index>) as the risk-free rates, the Sharpe ratio turns negative. Figure 9 plots the performance of this broad factor index from inception, without charging for the above costs (a)–(d). After more than fifteen years of out-of-sample performance, factor investing's Sharpe ratio is statistically insignificant at any reasonable rejection threshold.

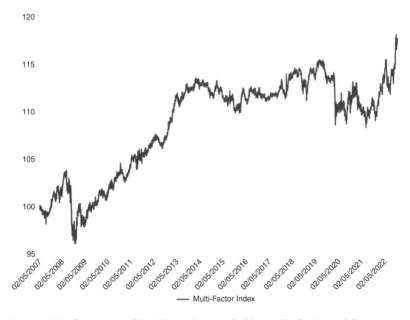

Figure 9 Performance of the Bloomberg – Goldman Sachs Asset Management US Equity Multi-Factor Index, since index inception (base 100 on May 2, 2007)

It takes over 31 years of daily observations for an investment strategy with an annualized Sharpe ratio of 0.29 to become statistically significant at a 95 percent confidence level (see Bailey and López de Prado (2012) for details of this calculation). If the present Sharpe ratio does not decay (e.g., due to overcrowding, or hedge funds preempting factor portfolio rebalances), researchers will have to wait until the year 2039 to reject the null hypothesis that factor investing is unprofitable, and even then, they will be earning a gross annual return of 1.13 percent before paying for costs (a)–(d).

There is a profound disconnect between the unwavering conviction expressed by academic authors and the underwhelming performance experienced by factor investors. A root cause of this disconnect is that factor investing studies usually make spurious claims, of two distinct types.

6.4.1 Type-A Spuriosity

I define an empirical claim to be of type-A spurious when a researcher mistakes random variability (noise) for signal, resulting in a false association. Selection bias under multiple testing is a leading cause for type-A spuriosity. Type-A spuriosity has several distinct attributes: (a) it results in type-1 errors (false positives); (b) for the same number of trials, it has a lower probability to take place as the sample size grows (López de Prado 2022b); and (c) it can be corrected through multiple-testing adjustments, such as Hochberg (1988) or Bailey and López de Prado (2014).

In the absence of serial correlation, the expected return of a type-A spurious investment factor is zero, before transaction costs and fees (Bailey et al. 2014). Next, I discuss the two main reasons for type-A spuriosity in the factor investing literature.

6.4.1.1 P-Hacking

The procedures inspired by Fama and MacBeth (1973) and Fama and French (1993) involve a large number of subjective decisions, such as fit window length, fit frequency, number of quantiles, definition of long-short portfolios, choice of controls, choice of factors, choice of investment universe, data cleaning and outlier removal decisions, start and end dates, etc. There are millions of potential combinations to pick from, many of which could be defended on logical grounds. Factor researchers routinely run multiple regressions before selecting a model with p-values below their null-rejection threshold. Authors report those minimal p-values without adjusting for selection bias under multiple testing, a malpractice known as p-hacking. The problem is compounded by publication bias, whereby journals accept papers without accounting for: (a) the number of previously rejected papers; and (b) the number of previously accepted papers. Harvey et al. (2016) conclude that "most claimed research findings in financial economics are likely false." The consequence is, factor investments do not perform as expected, and results are not replicated out-of-sample.

Other fields of research have addressed *p*-hacking decades ago. Statisticians have developed methods to determine the familywise error rate (Hochberg 1988; White 2000; Romano and Wolf 2005) and false discovery rate (Benjamini and Hochberg 1995).[31] Medical journals routinely demand the logging, reporting, and adjustment of results from all trials. Since 2008, laboratories are required by U.S. law to publish the results from all trials within a year of completion of a clinical study (Section 801 of the Food and Drug Administration Amendments Act of 2007).

While most disciplines are taking action to tackle the replication crisis, the majority of members of the factor investing research community remain unwaveringly committed to *p*-hacking. There are two possible explanations for their choice: ignorance and malpractice. Factor researchers have not been trained to control for multiple testing. To this day, all major econometrics textbooks fail to discuss solutions to the problem of conducting inference when more than one trial has taken place. As Harvey (2017, p. 1402) lamented, "*our* standard testing methods are often ill equipped to answer the questions that we pose. Other fields have thought deeply about testing" (emphasis added). However, ignorance alone does not explain why some factor investing authors argue that multiple testing is not a problem, against the advice of mathematical societies (Wasserstein and Lazar 2016). Harvey (2022) explains the stance of *p*-hacking deniers by pointing at the commercial interests that control financial academia.

6.4.1.2 Backtest Overfitting

A backtest is commonly defined as a historical simulation of how a systematic strategy would have performed in the past (López de Prado 2018, chapter 11). Factor researchers often present backtests as evidence that a claimed causal effect is real. However, a backtest is neither a controlled experiment, nor an RCT, nor a natural experiment, because it does not allow the researcher to intervene on the data-generating process (a do-operation), and a simulation does not involve the researcher's or Nature's random assignment of units to groups. Accordingly, a backtest has no power to prove or disprove a causal mechanism. At best, a backtest informs investors of the economic potential of an investment strategy,

---

[31] For an introduction to the concepts of familywise error rate and false discovery rate, see Efron and Hastie (2021, chapter 15).

under the assumption that history repeats itself (a distributional inductive belief, hence associational and noncausal).

Factor researchers rarely report or adjust for the number of trials involved in a backtest (Fabozzi and López de Prado 2018; López de Prado and Lewis 2019; López de Prado 2019). As demonstrated by the False Strategy Theorem, it is trivial to overfit a backtest through selection bias under multiple testing, making it hard to separate signal from noise (Bailey et al. 2014; Bailey and López de Prado 2014, 2021).

The outcome from a backtest is yet another associational claim. Replicating that associational claim does not prove that the association is causal, or that the noncausal association is true. Two researchers can independently mistake the same noise for signal, particularly when they narrow their modeling choices to linear regressions with similar biases. Obtaining similar backtest results on different sets of securities (e.g., from a different sector, or geography, or time period) does not constitute causal evidence, as those findings can be explained in terms of the same noncausal association being present on the chosen sets, or in terms of a statistical fluke.

6.4.2 Type-B Spuriosity

An association is true if it is not type-A spurious, however that does not mean that the association is causal. I define an empirical claim to be type-B spurious when a researcher mistakes association for causation. A leading cause for type-B spuriosity is systematic biases due to misspecification errors. A model is mis-specified when its functional form is incongruent with the functional form of the data-generating process, and the role played by the variables involved. Type-B spuriosity has several distinct attributes: (a) it results in type-1 errors and type-2 errors (false positives and false negatives); (b) it can occur with a single trial; (c) it has a greater probability to take place as the sample size grows, because the noncausal association can be estimated with lower error; and (d) it cannot be corrected through multiple-testing adjustments. Its correction requires the injection of extra-statistical information, in the form of a causal theory.

The expected return of a type-B spurious investment factor is misattributed, as a result of the biased estimates. Also, type-B spurious investment factors can exhibit time-varying risk premia (more on this in Section 6.4.2.1).

Type-A and type-B spuriosity are mutually exclusive. For type-B spuriosity to take place, the association must be noncausal but true, which precludes that association from being type-A spurious. While type-A spuriosity has been studied with some depth in the factor investing literature, relatively little has been written about type-B spuriosity. Next, I discuss the main reasons for type-B spuriosity in factor investing.

6.4.2.1 Under-Controlling

Consider a data-generating process where one of its equations is $Y := X\beta + Z\gamma + u$, such that $\gamma \neq 0$ and u is white noise. The process is unknown to a researcher, who attempts to estimate the causal effect of X on Y by fitting the equation $Y = X\beta + \varepsilon$ on a sample $\{X_t, Y_t\}_{t=1,\dots,T}$ produced by the process. This incorrect specification choice makes $\varepsilon = Z\gamma + u$, and $E[\varepsilon|X] = E[Z\gamma + u|X] = \gamma E[Z|X]$. However, if Z is correlated with X, $E[Z|X] \neq 0$, hence $E[\varepsilon|X] \neq 0$. This is a problem, because the least-squares method assumes $E[\varepsilon|X] = 0$ (the exogeneity assumption, see Section 5.2). Missing one or several relevant variables biases the estimate of β, potentially leading to spurious claims of causality. A false positive occurs when $|\hat{\beta}| \gg 0$ for $\beta \approx 0$, and a false negative occurs when $\hat{\beta} \approx 0$ for $|\beta| \gg 0$.

Econometrics textbooks do not distinguish between types of missing variables (see, for example, Greene 2012, section 4.3.2), yet not all missing variables are created equal. There are two distinct cases that researchers must consider. In the first case, the second equation of the data-generating process is $Z := X\delta + v$, where $\delta \neq 0$ and v is white noise. In this case, Z is a mediator (X causes Z, and Z causes Y), and the chosen specification biases the estimation of the direct effect $\hat{\beta}$; however, $\hat{\beta}$ can still be interpreted as a total causal effect (through two causal paths with the same origin and end). The causal graph for this first case is displayed at the top of Figure 10. In the second case, the second equation of the data-generating process is $X := Z\delta + v$, where $\delta \neq 0$ and v is white noise. In this case, Z is a confounder (Z causes X and Y), the chosen specification also biases $\hat{\beta}$, and $\hat{\beta}$ does not measure a causal effect (whether total or direct).[32] The causal graph for this second case is displayed at the bottom of Figure 10.

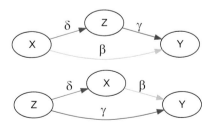

Figure 10 Variable Z as mediator (top) and confounder (bottom)

Assuming that the white noise is Gaussian, the expression $E[\hat{\beta}|X]$ reduces to

$$E[\hat{\beta}|X] = (X'X)^{-1}X'E[X\beta + Z\gamma + u|X] =$$

$$\beta + \gamma\delta(1 + \delta^2)^{-1} = \beta + \theta \tag{16}$$

where $\theta = \gamma\delta(1 + \delta^2)^{-1}$ is the bias due to the missing confounder. The Appendix contains a proof of the above proposition. The intuition behind θ is that a necessary and sufficient condition for a biased estimate of β is that $\gamma \neq 0$ and $\delta \neq 0$, because when both parameters are nonzero, variable Z is a confounder.

A first consequence of missing a confounder is incorrect performance attribution and risk management. Part of the performance experienced by the investor comes from a misattributed risk characteristic Z, which should have been hedged by a correctly specified model. The investor is exposed to both, causal association (from β), as intended by the model's specification, and noncausal association (from θ), which is not intended by the model's specification.

A second consequence of missing a confounder is time-varying risk premia. Consider the case where the market rewards exposure to X and Z ($\beta > 0$, $\gamma > 0$). Even if the two risk premia remain constant, changes over time in δ will change $\hat{\beta}$. In particular, for a sufficiently negative value of δ, then $\hat{\beta} < 0$. Performance misattribution will mislead investors into believing that the market has turned to punish exposure to risk characteristic X, when in reality their losses have nothing to do with changes in risk premia. The culprit is a change in the covariance between the intended exposure (X) and the unintended exposure that should have been hedged (Z). Authors explain time-varying risk premia as the result to changes in expected market returns (e.g., Evans 1994; Anderson 2011; and Cochrane 2011), and asset managers' marketing departments justify their underperformance in terms of temporary changes in investor or market behavior. While these explanations are plausible, they seem to ignore that time-varying risk premia is consistent with a missing confounder (an arguably more likely and parsimonious, hence preferable, explanation). For example, consider the causal graph in Figure 8, where MOM confounds the estimate of the effect of HML on PC. If an asset manager under-controls for MOM, the value investment strategy will be exposed to changes in the covariance between MOM and HML. The asset manager may tell investors that the value strategy is losing money because of a change in value's risk premium, when the correct explanation is that the product is defective, as a result of under-controlling. Changes in the covariance between MOM and HML have nothing to do with value's or momentum's true risk premia, which remain unchanged (like the direct causal effects, HML → PC and MOM → PC). This flaw of type-B spurious factor investing strategies makes them untrustworthy.

The *partial correlations method* allows researchers to control for observable confounders when the causal effect is linear and the random variables jointly follow an elliptical (including multivariate normal) distribution, multivariate hypergeometric distribution, multivariate negative hypergeometric distribution, multinomial distribution, or Dirichlet distribution (Baba et al. 2004). A researcher is said to "control" for the confounding effect of Z when he adds Z as a regressor in an equation set to model the effect of X on Y. Accordingly, the new model specification for estimating the effect of X on Y is $Y = X\beta + Z\gamma + \varepsilon$. This is a particular application of the more general backdoor adjustment (Section 4.3.2.2), and by far the most common confounder bias correction method used in regression analysis. This adjustment method relies on a linear regression, thus inheriting its assumptions and limitations. In particular, the partial correlations method is not robust when the explanatory variables exhibit high correlation (positive or negative) with each other (multicollinearity).

6.4.2.2 Over-Controlling

The previous section explained the negative consequences of under-controlling (e.g., missing a confounder). However, over-controlling is not less pernicious. Statisticians have been trained for decades to control for any variable Z associated with Y that is not X (Pearl and MacKenzie 2018, pp. 139, 152, 154, 163), regardless of the role of Z in the causal graph (the so-called omitted variable problem). Econometrics textbooks dismiss as a harmless error the inclusion of an irrelevant variable, regardless of the variable's role in the causal graph. For example, Greene (2012, section 4.3.3) states that the only downside to adding superfluous variables is a reduction in the precision of the estimates. This grave misunderstanding has certainly led to countless type-B spurious claims in economics.

In recent years, do-calculus has revealed that some variables should not be controlled for, even if they are associated with Y. Figure 11 shows two examples of causal graphs where controlling for Z will lead to biased estimates of the effect of X on Y.

Common examples of over-controlling include controlling for variables that are mediators or colliders relative to the causal path from X to Y.[33] Controlling for a collider is a mistake, as it opens a backdoor path that biases the effect's

---

[33] In the words of Pearl and MacKenzie (2018, p. 276): "[M]istaking a mediator for a confounder is one of the deadliest sins in causal inference and may lead to the most outrageous errors. The latter invited adjustment; the former forbids it."

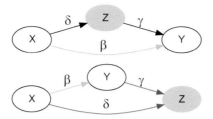

Figure 11 Variable Z as controlled mediator (top) and controlled collider (bottom)

estimation (Berkson's fallacy, see Berkson 1946). Controlling for a mediator interferes with the mediated effect $(X \rightarrow Z \rightarrow Y)$ and the total causal effect $(X \rightarrow Z \rightarrow Y$ plus $X \rightarrow Y)$ that the researcher may wish to assess, leaving only the direct effect $X \rightarrow Y$. In the case of the top causal graph in Figure 11, a researcher could estimate the mediated effect $X \rightarrow Z \rightarrow Y$ as the difference between the total effect $(X \rightarrow Z \rightarrow Y$ plus $X \rightarrow Y)$ and the direct effect $(X \rightarrow Y)$.

Over-controlling a collider and under-controlling a confounder have the same impact on the causal graph: allowing the flow of association through a backdoor path (Section 4.3.2.2). Consequently, over-controlled models can suffer from the same conditions as under-controlled models, namely (i) biased estimates, as a result of noncompliance with the exogeneity assumption; and (ii) time-varying risk premia. Black-box investment strategies take over-controlling to the extreme. Over-controlling explains why quantitative funds that deploy black-box investment strategies routinely transition from delivering systematic profits to delivering systematic losses, and there is not much fund managers or investors can do to detect that transition until it is too late.

The only way to determine precisely which variables a researcher must control for, in order to block (or keep blocked) noncausal paths of association, is through the careful analysis of a causal graph (e.g., front-door criterion and backdoor criterion). The problem is, factor researchers almost never estimate or declare the causal graphs associated with the phenomenon under study (Section 6.2). Odds are, factor researchers have severely biased their estimates of β by controlling for the wrong variables, which in turn has led to false positives and false negatives.

6.4.2.3 Specification-Searching

Specification-searching is the popular practice among factor researchers of choosing a model's specification (including the selection of variables and functional forms) based on the resulting model's explanatory power. To cite one example, consider the three-factor model introduced by Fama and French (1993), and the five-factor model introduced by Fama and French (2015). Fama and French

(2015)'s argument for adding two factors to their initial model specification was that "the five-factor model performs better than the three-factor model when used to explain average returns."

These authors' line of argumentation is self-contradictory. The use of explanatory power (an associational, noncausal concept) for selecting the specification of a predictive model is consistent with the associational goal of that analysis; however, it is at odds with the causal content of a factor model. In the context of factor models, specification-searching commingles two separate and sequential stages of the causal analysis: (1) causal discovery (Section 4.3.1); and (2) control (Section 4.3.2). Stage (2) should be informed by stage (1), not the other way around. Unlike a causal graph, a coefficient of determination cannot convey the extra-statistical information needed to de-confound the estimate of a causal effect, hence the importance of keeping stages (1) and (2) separate.

Stage (1) discovers the causal graph that best explains the phenomenon as a whole, including observational evidence and extra-statistical information. In stage (2), given the discovered causal graph, the specification of a factor model should be informed exclusively by the aim to estimate *one* of the causal effects (one of the arrows or causal paths) declared in the causal graph, applying the tools of do-calculus. In a causal model, the correct specification is not the one that predicts Y best, but the one that debiases $\hat{\beta}$ best, for a single treatment variable, in agreement with the causal graph. Choosing a factor model's specification based on its explanatory power incurs the risk of biasing the estimated causal effects. For example, a researcher may achieve higher explanatory power by combining multiple causes of Y, at the expense of biasing the multiple parameters' estimates due to multicollinearity or over-controlling for a collider.[34] It is easy to find realistic causal structures where specification-searching leads to false positives, and misspecified factor models that misattribute risk and performance (see Section 7.3).

There are two possible counter-arguments to the above reasoning: (a) A researcher may want to combine multiple causes of Y in an attempt to model an interaction effect. However, such attempt is a stage (2) analysis that should be justified with the causal graph derived from stage (1), showing that the total effect involves several variables that are observed separately, but that need to be modeled jointly; and (b) a researcher may want to show that the two causes are not mutually redundant (a multifactor explanation, see Fama and French 1996). However, there exist far more sophisticated tools for

---

[34] When the Gauss-Markov assumptions hold, multicollinearity does not introduce bias, and it only inflates standard errors. However, when those assumptions do not hold, multicollinearity can amplify the bias introduced by a misspecified model (Kalnins, 2022).

making that case, such as mutual information or variation of information analyses (López de Prado 2020, chapter 3).

While specification-searching may involve multiple testing, specification-searching is not addressed by multiple testing corrections, as it has to do with the proper modeling of causal relationships, regardless of the number of trials involved in improving the model's explanatory power. Accordingly, specification-searching is a source of spuriosity that is distinct from *p*-hacking, and whose consequence is specification bias rather than selection bias. As argued in an earlier section, investors interested in predictive power should apply machine learning algorithms, which model association, not causation.

6.4.2.4 Failure to Account for Temporal Properties

In the context of time-series analysis, two independent variables may appear to be associated when: (a) their time series are nonstationary (Granger and Newbold 1974); and (b) their time series are stationary, however they exhibit strong temporal properties, such as positively autocorrelated autoregressive series or long moving averages (Granger et al. 2001). This occurs regardless of the sample size and for various distributions of the error terms.

Unit root and cointegration analyses help address concerns regarding the distribution of residuals, however they cannot help mitigate the risk of making type-B spurious claims. Like their cross-sectional counterparts, time-series models also require proper model specification through causal analysis, as discussed in the earlier sections. Section 5.3 exemplified one way in which econometricians mistake association for causation in time-series models.

6.5 Hierarchy of Evidence

Not all types of empirical evidence presented in support of a scientific claim are equally strong. The reason is, some types of evidence are more susceptible to being spurious than other types. Figure 12 ranks the types of empirical evidence often used in financial research, in accordance with their scientific rigor. Categories colored in red support associational claims, and hence are phenomenological. Categories colored in green make use of the formal language of causal inference, hence enabling the statistical falsification of a causal claim (see Section 3.4).

At the bottom of the hierarchy is the expert opinion, such as the discretionary view of an investment guru, which relies on rules of thumb and educated guesses (heuristics) to reach a conclusion. A case study proposes a rationale to explain multiple aspects of a phenomenon (variative induction), however it typically lacks academic rigor and suffers from confirmation or selection biases. An econometric (observational) study, such as an investment factor model or

Rank	Type	Inference	Rigor	Example
1	Randomized controlled trials	Deduction (with partial induction)	Very high	Algo-wheel experiments (e.g., Section 3.3)
2	Natural experiments	Deduction (with weak assumptions)	High	Market-maker reaction to random spikes in order imbalance (e.g., Section 3.3)
3	Simulated interventions	Deduction (with strong assumptions)	Medium	Estimate effect of HML using a causal graph (e.g., Section 6.2.1)
4	Econometric (observational) studies	Enumerative induction	Low	Factor investing literature; backtested investment strategies (e.g., Section 6.4.1)
5	Case studies	Variative induction	Very low	Broker report / analysis
6	Expert opinion	Heuristic	Anecdotal	Investment guru's prediction

Figure 12 Hierarchy of evidence in financial research, ranked by scientific rigor

backtest, relies primarily on statistical patterns observed on numerous instances (enumerative induction). Econometric studies can be academically rigorous, however they are afflicted by the pitfalls explained in Section 6.4. These three associational types of evidence are highly susceptible to type-A and type-B spuriosity.

A simulated intervention is qualitatively different from the bottom three categories because it uses the formal language of causal inference to communicate a falsifiable theory. The deduced causal effects rely on the strong assumption that the causal graph is correct.[35] Natural experiments are yet superior to simulated experiments because the former involve an actual do-operation. The deduced causal effects rely on the weaker assumption that Nature's assignment of units to the treatment and control groups has been random. Finally, the top spot belongs to RCTs, because they offer the greatest level of transparency and reproducibility. The deduced causal effects rely on the assumption that the underlying causal mechanism will continue to operate (a form of induction). At the present, controlled experiments on financial systems are not possible, due to

---

[35] I use here the term "strong assumption" to denote assumptions whose validity implies the validity of other (weaker) assumptions. However, the validity of weak assumptions does not imply the validity of strong assumptions. For example, the validity of a causal graph is a strong assumption that implies weaker assumptions, such as invariance, stationarity, and ergodicity.

the complexity of these systems, but also due to ethical and regulatory considerations.

The reader should not conclude from Figure 12 that associational evidence is useless. As explained in Section 3.1, associations play a critical role in the phenomenological step of the scientific method. Furthermore, the causal mechanism embedded in a theory implies the existence of key associations which, if not found, falsify the theory (see Section 3.3). In standard sequent notation, the claim that $C \Rightarrow A$ is not enough to assert $A \Rightarrow C$, however it is enough to assert that $\neg A \Rightarrow \neg C$, where C stands for causation and A stands for association. The reason is, causation is a special kind of association (i.e., the kind that flows through a causal path), hence the absence of association is enough to debunk the claim of causation by *modus tollens*.

Figure 12 does not include out-of-sample evidence as a category, because "out-of-sample" is not a type of causal evidence but rather a description of when the data was collected or used. Evidence collected out-of-sample is of course preferable to evidence collected in-sample, as the former is more resilient to type-A spuriosity, however evidence collected out-of-sample is not necessarily more resilient to type-B spuriosity. For example, a researcher may collect out-of-sample evidence of the correlation between stocks and bonds, and from that measurement be tempted to deduce that changes in one's price cause changes in the other's price. While a causal link between stocks and bonds would be a possible explanation for the observed association, the existence of correlation does not suffice to claim a direct causal relationship, regardless of whether the measurement was taken in-sample or out-of-sample.

7 Monte Carlo Experiments

As explained in Section 6.4.2, factor model specification errors can lead to false positives and false negatives. This section presents three instances of causal structures where the application of standard econometric procedures leads to mistaking association with causation, and ultimately to type-B spurious factor claims. Standard econometric procedures are expected to perform equally poorly on more complex causal structures.

7.1 Fork

Three variables $\{X, Y, Z\}$ form a fork when variable Z is a direct cause of variable X and variable Y (see Figure 13). Consider a researcher who wishes to model Y as a function of X. In that case, Z is said to be a confounding variable because not controlling for the effect of Z on X and Y will bias the estimation of the effect of X on Y. Given a probability distribution P, the application of Bayesian network factorization on the fork represented by Figure 13 yields[36]:

$$P[X, Y, Z] = P[Z]P[X|Z]P[Y|Z] \tag{17}$$

which implies a (noncausal) association between X and Y, since

$$P[X, Y] = \sum_{Z} P[Z]P[X|Z]P[Y|Z] \neq P[X]P[Y]. \tag{18}$$

This is an example of noncausal association, because X and Y are associated through the backdoor path $Y \leftarrow Z \rightarrow X$, even though there is no causal path between X and Y. The effect of conditioning by Z is equivalent to simulating a do-operation (an intervention), because it blocks the backdoor path, resulting in the conditional independence of X and Y,

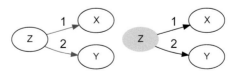

Figure 13 Causal graph with a confounder Z, before (left) and after (right) control

---

[36] For an introduction to the calculus of Bayesian network factorization, see Pearl et al. (2016, pp. 29–32) and Neal (2020, pp. 20–22).

$$P[X, Y|Z] = \frac{P[X, Y, Z]}{P[Z]} = P[X|Z]P[Y|Z]. \tag{19}$$

Conditioning by variable Z de-confounds $P[X, Y]$ in this causal graph, however not in other causal graphs. The widespread notion that econometricians should condition (or control) for all variables involved in a phenomenon is misleading, as explained in Section 6.4.2.2. The precise de-confounding variables are determined by do-calculus rules (see Section 4.3.2). The above conclusions can be verified through the following numerical experiment. First, draw 5,000 observations from the data-generating process characterized by the structural equation model,

$$Z_t := \xi_t \tag{20}$$

$$X_t := Z_t + \epsilon_t \tag{21}$$

$$Y_t := Z_t + \zeta_t \tag{22}$$

where $\{\xi_t, \epsilon_t, \zeta_t\}$ are three independent random variables that follow a standard Normal distribution. Second, fit on the 5,000 observations the linear equation,

$$Y_t = \alpha + \beta X_t + \varepsilon_t. \tag{23}$$

Figure 14 reports the results of the least-squares estimate. Following the econometric canon, a researcher will conclude that $\hat{\beta}$ is statistically significant.

```
                          OLS Regression Results
===============================================================================
Dep. Variable:                      Y   R-squared:                      0.247
Model:                            OLS   Adj. R-squared:                 0.247
Method:                 Least Squares   F-statistic:                     1640.
Date:                Sun, 14 Aug 2022   Prob (F-statistic):          2.69e-310
Time:                        13:14:32   Log-Likelihood:                -8052.6
No. Observations:                5000   AIC:                         1.611e+04
Df Residuals:                    4998   BIC:                         1.612e+04
Df Model:                           1
Covariance Type:            nonrobust
===============================================================================
                 coef    std err          t      P>|t|     [0.025      0.975]
-------------------------------------------------------------------------------
const          0.0090      0.017      0.524      0.600     -0.025       0.043
X              0.4964      0.012     40.493      0.000      0.472       0.520
===============================================================================
Omnibus:                        1.784   Durbin-Watson:                  1.964
Prob(Omnibus):                  0.410   Jarque-Bera (JB):               1.746
Skew:                           0.027   Prob(JB):                       0.418
Kurtosis:                       3.073   Cond. No.                       1.40
===============================================================================
```

Figure 14 False positive due to missing confounder Z

Given the causal content injected by the researcher through the least-squares model specification, a statistically significant $\hat{\beta}$ implies the statement "X causes Y," not the statement "X is associated with Y" (Section 5.2). If the researcher intended to establish association, he should have used an associational model, such as Pearson's correlation coefficient, or orthogonal regression (Section 5.1). At the same time, Figure 13 shows that there is no causal path from X to Y. The claim of statistical significance is type-B spurious because Y is not a function of X, as implied by the model's specification. This is the effect of missing a single confounder.

As explained in Section 6.4.2.1, it is possible to remove the confounder-induced bias by adding Z as a regressor (the partial correlations method),

$$Y_t = \alpha + \beta X_t + \gamma Z_t + \varepsilon_t \tag{24}$$

Figure 15 reports the result of this adjustment. With the correct model specification, the researcher will conclude that X does not cause Y. The code for this experiment can be found in the Appendix.

7.2 Immorality

Three variables $\{X, Y, Z\}$ form an immorality when variable Z is directly caused by variable X and variable Y (see Figure 16). Consider a researcher who wishes to model Y as a function of X. In that case, Z is said to be a collider variable.

```
                          OLS Regression Results
==============================================================================
Dep. Variable:                   Y    R-squared:                     0.495
Model:                         OLS    Adj. R-squared:                0.495
Method:              Least Squares    F-statistic:                   2447.
Date:             Sun, 14 Aug 2022    Prob (F-statistic):             0.00
Time:                     13:14:32    Log-Likelihood:              -7054.9
No. Observations:             5000    AIC:                       1.412e+04
Df Residuals:                 4997    BIC:                       1.414e+04
Df Model:                        2
Covariance Type:         nonrobust
==============================================================================
                 coef    std err          t      P>|t|      [0.025      0.975]
------------------------------------------------------------------------------
const          0.0054      0.014      0.383      0.702      -0.022       0.033
X              0.0007      0.014      0.051      0.959      -0.027       0.029
Z              0.9957      0.020     49.506      0.000       0.956       1.035
==============================================================================
Omnibus:                       2.685   Durbin-Watson:                   1.972
Prob(Omnibus):                 0.261   Jarque-Bera (JB):                2.629
Skew:                          0.050   Prob(JB):                        0.269
Kurtosis:                      3.050   Cond. No.                         2.62
==============================================================================
```

Figure 15 De-confounding through the partial correlations method

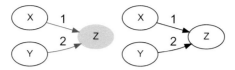

Figure 16 Causal graph with a collider Z, with (left) and without (right) control

Colliders should be particularly concerning to econometricians because controlling for the effect of Z on X and Y biases the estimation of the effect of X on Y. Given a probability distribution P, the application of Bayesian network factorization on the immorality represented by Figure 16 yields:

$$P[X, Y, Z] = P[X]P[Y]P[Z|X, Y]. \tag{25}$$

There is no association between X and Y because

$$P[X, Y] = \sum_Z P[X]P[Y]P[Z|X, Y] = P[X]P[Y] \sum_Z P[Z|X, Y] = P[X]P[Y]. \tag{26}$$

However, conditioning on Z opens the backdoor path between X and Y that Z was blocking $(Y \rightarrow Z \leftarrow X)$. The following analytical example illustrates this fact. Consider the data-generating process

$$X_t := \epsilon_t \tag{27}$$

$$Y_t := \zeta_t \tag{28}$$

$$Z_t := X_t + Y_t + \xi_t \tag{29}$$

where $\{\xi_t, \epsilon_t, \zeta_t\}$ are three independent random variables that follow a standard Normal distribution. Then, the covariance between X and Y is

$$Cov[X, Y] = E[(X - E[X])(Y - E[Y])] = E[XY] = E[X]E[Y] = 0 \tag{30}$$

The problem is, a researcher who (wrongly) conditions on Z will find a negative covariance between X and Y, even though there is no causal path between X and Y, because

$$Cov[X, Y|Z] = -\frac{1}{3} \tag{31}$$

The Appendix contains a proof of the above proposition. Compare the causal graph in Figure 16 with the causal graph in Figure 13. Figure 13 has a structure $X \leftarrow Z \rightarrow Y$, where not controlling for confounder Z results in under-controlling.

The direction of causality is reversed in Figure 16, transforming the confounder into a collider. In the structure $X \rightarrow Z \leftarrow Y$, controlling for Z results in over-controlling. This is an instance of Berkson's fallacy, whereby a noncausal association is observed between two independent variables, as a result of conditioning on a collider (Pearl 2009, p. 17).

This finding is problematic for econometricians because the direction of causality cannot always be solely determined by observational studies (Peters et al. 2017, pp. 44–45), and solving the confounder-collider conundrum often requires the injection of extra-statistical (beyond observational) information. Causal graphs inject the required extra-statistical information, by making explicit assumptions that complement the information contributed by observations.[37] Accordingly, the statistical and econometric mantra "data speaks for itself" is in fact misleading, because two econometricians who rely solely on observational evidence can consistently reach contradicting conclusions from the analysis of the same data. With a careful selection of colliders, a researcher can present evidence in support of any type-B spurious investment factor. The correct causal treatment of a collider is to indicate its presence and explain why researchers should not control for it. A key takeaway is that researchers must declare and justify the hypothesized causal graph that supports their chosen model specification, or else submit to the healthy skepticism of their peers.

We can verify the above conclusions with the following numerical experiment. First, draw 5,000 observations from the above data-generating process. Second, fit on the 5,000 observations the linear equation

$$Y_t = \alpha + \beta X_t + \gamma Z_t + \varepsilon_t \tag{32}$$

Figure 17 reports the results of the least-squares estimate. Following the econometric canon, a researcher will conclude that $\hat{\beta}$ is statistically significant. This claim of statistical significance is type-B spurious because Y is not a function of X, as implied by the model's specification. This is the effect of controlling for a collider.

We can remove the bias induced by collider Z by excluding that variable from the model's specification,

$$Y_t = \alpha + \beta X_t + \varepsilon_t \tag{33}$$

---

[37] In the absence of an interventional study or a natural experiment, the statement X causes Y is an assumption, which may be consistent with, however not proved by, observational evidence (Section 4.3).

```
                        OLS Regression Results
==============================================================================
Dep. Variable:                    Y   R-squared:                       0.499
Model:                          OLS   Adj. R-squared:                  0.499
Method:               Least Squares   F-statistic:                     2490.
Date:              Sun, 14 Aug 2022   Prob (F-statistic):               0.00
Time:                      13:11:51   Log-Likelihood:                -5314.4
No. Observations:              5000   AIC:                         1.063e+04
Df Residuals:                  4997   BIC:                         1.065e+04
Df Model:                         2
Covariance Type:          nonrobust
==============================================================================
                 coef    std err          t      P>|t|      [0.025      0.975]
------------------------------------------------------------------------------
const         -0.0138      0.010     -1.388      0.165      -0.033       0.006
X             -0.4963      0.012    -40.405      0.000      -0.520      -0.472
Z              0.4988      0.007     70.575      0.000       0.485       0.513
==============================================================================
Omnibus:                        0.058   Durbin-Watson:                   1.998
Prob(Omnibus):                  0.971   Jarque-Bera (JB):                0.037
Skew:                           0.001   Prob(JB):                        0.982
Kurtosis:                       3.013   Cond. No.                         2.41
==============================================================================
```

Figure 17 False positive due to adding collider Z

```
                        OLS Regression Results
==============================================================================
Dep. Variable:                    Y   R-squared:                       0.000
Model:                          OLS   Adj. R-squared:                 -0.000
Method:               Least Squares   F-statistic:                   0.01120
Date:              Sun, 14 Aug 2022   Prob (F-statistic):              0.916
Time:                      13:11:51   Log-Likelihood:                -7043.2
No. Observations:              5000   AIC:                         1.409e+04
Df Residuals:                  4998   BIC:                         1.410e+04
Df Model:                         1
Covariance Type:          nonrobust
==============================================================================
                 coef    std err          t      P>|t|      [0.025      0.975]
------------------------------------------------------------------------------
const         -0.0221      0.014     -1.580      0.114      -0.050       0.005
X              0.0015      0.014      0.106      0.916      -0.026       0.029
==============================================================================
Omnibus:                        0.633   Durbin-Watson:                   1.998
Prob(Omnibus):                  0.729   Jarque-Bera (JB):                0.638
Skew:                           0.028   Prob(JB):                        0.727
Kurtosis:                       2.994   Cond. No.                         1.02
==============================================================================
```

Figure 18 Debiasing by removing collider Z

Figure 18 reports the results of this adjustment. Note that the misspecified model delivered higher explanatory power, hence specification-searching would have misled the researcher into a false positive. With the correct model specification, the researcher will conclude that X does not cause Y. The code for this experiment can be found in the Appendix.

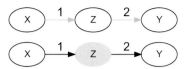

Figure 19 Causal graph with mediator Z, before (top)
and after (bottom) control

7.3 Chain

Three variables $\{X, Y, Z\}$ form a chain when variable Z mediates the causal flow from variable X to variable Y (see Figure 19). Consider a researcher who wishes to model Y as a function of X. In that case, Z is said to be a mediator variable.

Given a probability distribution P, the application of Bayesian network factorization on the chain represented by Figure 19 yields:

$$P[X, Y, Z] = P[X]P[Z|X]P[Y|Z] \tag{34}$$

which implies an association between X and Y, since

$$P[X, Y] = \sum_Z P[X]P[Z|X]P[Y|Z] \neq P[X]P[Y] \tag{35}$$

There is no backdoor path in Figure 19. This is an example of association with causation, because X and Y are associated only through the causal path mediated by Z. Like in the case of a fork, the effect of conditioning by Z is equivalent to simulating a do-operation (an intervention), resulting in the conditional independence of X and Y,

$$P[X, Y|Z] = \frac{P[X, Y, Z]}{P[Z]} = \frac{P[X]P[Z|X]P[Y|Z]}{P[Z]} = \frac{P[X, Z]}{P[Z]}P[Y|Z] = P[X|Z]P[Y|Z] \tag{36}$$

The problem with conditioning on a mediator is that it may disrupt the very causal association that the researcher wants to estimate (an instance of over-controlling, see Section 6.4.2.2), leading to a false negative. Making matters more complex, conditioning on a mediator can also lead to a false positive. This statement can be verified through the following numerical experiment. First, draw 5,000 observations from the data-generating process characterized by the structural equation model

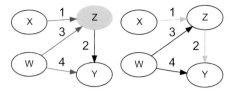

Figure 20 A confounded mediator (Z), with (left) and without (right) control

$$X_t := \epsilon_t \tag{37}$$

$$W_t := \eta_t \tag{38}$$

$$Z_t := X_t + W_t + \xi_t \tag{39}$$

$$Y_t := Z_t + W_t + \zeta_t \tag{40}$$

where $\{\xi_t, \epsilon_t, \zeta_t, \eta_t\}$ are four independent random variables that follow a standard Normal distribution. Figure 20 displays the relevant causal graph.[38] Second, fit on the 5,000 observations the linear equation

$$Y_t = \alpha + \beta X_t + \gamma Z_t + \varepsilon_t. \tag{41}$$

Figure 21 reports the results of the least-squares estimate. While it is true that X causes Y (through Z), this result is still a false positive, because the reported association did not flow through the causal path $X \rightarrow Z \rightarrow Y$. The reason is, Z also operates as a collider to X and W, and controlling for Z has opened the backdoor path $X \rightarrow Z \leftarrow W \rightarrow Y$. This is the reason $\hat{\beta} \ll 0$, despite of all effects being positive. This phenomenon is known as the *mediation fallacy*, which involves conditioning on the mediator when the mediator and the outcome are confounded (Pearl and MacKenzie 2018, p. 315). This experiment also illustrates Simpson's paradox, which occurs when an association is observed in several groups of data, but it disappears or reverses when the groups are combined (Pearl et al. 2016, pp. 1–6).

Following the rules of do-calculus, the effect of X on Y in this causal graph can be estimated without controls. The reason is, the noncausal path through W is already blocked by Z. Controlling for W is not strictly necessary to debias $\hat{\beta}$, however it can help improve the precision of the estimates. The following model specification produces an unbiased estimate of β:

---

[38] The reader may find this diagram familiar, from Section 4.3.2.4. Should Z be the treatment variable, X would be an instrumental variable capable of de-confounding the effect of Z on Y from the bias introduced by W. However, in this case Z is a mediator, and X is the treatment variable, not an instrument.

```
                      OLS Regression Results
==============================================================================
Dep. Variable:                    Y   R-squared:                      0.784
Model:                          OLS   Adj. R-squared:                 0.784
Method:               Least Squares   F-statistic:                     9069.
Date:              Sun, 14 Aug 2022   Prob (F-statistic):              0.00
Time:                      13:04:29   Log-Likelihood:                -8061.9
No. Observations:              5000   AIC:                         1.613e+04
Df Residuals:                  4997   BIC:                         1.615e+04
Df Model:                         2
Covariance Type:          nonrobust
==============================================================================
                 coef    std err          t      P>|t|      [0.025      0.975]
------------------------------------------------------------------------------
const          0.0027      0.017      0.160      0.873      -0.031       0.036
X             -0.4814      0.021    -22.621      0.000      -0.523      -0.440
Z              1.4899      0.012    121.680      0.000       1.466       1.514
==============================================================================
Omnibus:                        0.314   Durbin-Watson:                  1.994
Prob(Omnibus):                  0.855   Jarque-Bera (JB):               0.267
Skew:                           0.000   Prob(JB):                       0.875
Kurtosis:                       3.036   Cond. No.                       2.41
==============================================================================
```

Figure 21 False positive due to adding a confounded mediator Z

```
                      OLS Regression Results
==============================================================================
Dep. Variable:                    Y   R-squared:                      0.144
Model:                          OLS   Adj. R-squared:                 0.144
Method:               Least Squares   F-statistic:                     840.8
Date:              Sun, 14 Aug 2022   Prob (F-statistic):          5.32e-171
Time:                      13:04:29   Log-Likelihood:                -11504.
No. Observations:              5000   AIC:                         2.301e+04
Df Residuals:                  4998   BIC:                         2.303e+04
Df Model:                         1
Covariance Type:          nonrobust
==============================================================================
                 coef    std err          t      P>|t|      [0.025      0.975]
------------------------------------------------------------------------------
const         -0.0222      0.034     -0.650      0.515      -0.089       0.045
X              1.0055      0.035     28.996      0.000       0.938       1.073
==============================================================================
Omnibus:                        0.250   Durbin-Watson:                  1.993
Prob(Omnibus):                  0.883   Jarque-Bera (JB):               0.288
Skew:                           0.009   Prob(JB):                       0.866
Kurtosis:                       2.968   Cond. No.                       1.02
==============================================================================
```

Figure 22 De-confounding by removing the confounded mediator

$$Y_t = \alpha + \beta X_t + \varepsilon_t \tag{42}$$

Figure 22 reports the results. Note that the correct model specification has much lower explanatory power: the adjusted R-squared drops from 0.784 to 0.144, and the F-statistic drops from 9,069 to 840.8. A specification-searching researcher would have chosen and reported the wrong model, because it has higher explanatory power, resulting in a misspecified model that misattributes risk and performance (Section 6.4.2.3).

With the proper model specification, as informed by the declared causal graph, the researcher correctly concludes that X causes Y, and that $\hat{\beta} \gg 0$. The code for this experiment can be found in the Appendix.

7.4 An Alternative Explanation for Factors

Consider the influential three-factor and five-factor models proposed by Fama and French (1993) and Fama and French (2015). These journal articles, henceforth referred to as FF93 and FF15 respectively, have inspired and served as template for thousands of academic papers purporting the discovery of hundreds of factors. FF93 postulates that the cross-section of average stock returns is partly explained by a linear function of three factors, namely the broad market, size (quantified as stock price times number of shares), and value (quantified as book-to-market equity). FF15 added to this mix two quality-inspired factors, profitability and investment, on the premise of improving the model's explanatory power. The model specifications proposed by FF93 and FF15 raise several objections: First, the authors fail to report and adjust for all the trials carried out before selecting their model, thus p-hacking has likely taken place (Section 6.4.1.1). Second, the authors justify the proposed specifications in terms of explanatory power, instead of a causal graph, thus the model is likely misspecified due to specification-searching (Section 6.4.2.3). Third, the authors ignore known macroeconomic confounders, such as inflation, GDP, stage of the business cycle, steepness of the yield curve, etc. Strangely, section 2.1.2 of FF93 makes explicit mention to the confounding effect of business cycles on size, and yet that confounder is inexplicably absent in the model. This points to a missing confounder (Section 6.4.2.1). Fourth, it is well documented that there is an interaction between the momentum and value factors (Barroso and Santa-Clara 2015). This interaction could be explained by a confounding relation between momentum and value, making momentum another likely missing confounding variable. Fifth, the authors do not provide the causal mechanism responsible for the reported observations, in denial of the causal content of their model, hence obstructing mediation analysis and falsification efforts (Section 6.3).

Carhart (1997) (henceforth C97) expanded FF93 by adding momentum as a fourth factor; however, the justification for that expansion was that the four-factor model achieved higher explanatory power (an associational argument), not that controlling for momentum de-confounded the estimate of value's causal effect. This is the same self-contradictory argument that FF15 used to add the two quality factors (Section 6.4.2.3). As demonstrated in Section 7.3, a correctly specified model can deliver lower explanatory power than a misspecified model on the same dataset. Improving on FF93's explanatory power does not make C97's model better specified, or its estimates less biased. Furthermore, the de-confounding control variable (momentum) is highly correlated with the confounded variable (value), thus exchanging confounder bias for multicollinearity. There are better ways of debiasing value's causal effect estimate. Instead of the partial correlations method, authors could apply the backdoor adjustment (or some other do-calculus adjustment), in order to avoid the multicollinearity caused by the inversion of that covariance matrix.

There is a plausible sixth objection to the specification of FF93, FF15, and C97. Suppose that (1) a company's stock returns and size are independent variables; and (2) both variables influence the company's book-to-market equity (a collider). In this case, as explained in Section 6.4.2.2 and illustrated in Section 7.2, conditioning on book-to-market equity introduces a negative noncausal association between the two independent variables in (1). In other words, by adding book-to-market equity to their model specification, FF93, FF15, and C97 may have inadvertently induced a noncausal negative correl ation between stock returns and size, making the size factor a false discovery.

The numerical experiments in Section 7 demonstrate that general causal structures can explain away the findings in FF93, FF15, and C97 as type-B spurious. Figure 23 provides an example of a causal graph under which the estimates in FF93, FF15, and C97 are biased by confounders and colliders. This particular graph may not be correct, however, the burden of proving it wrong belongs to the authors claiming the existence of investment factors. To address these concerns, those authors should make their models' causal content explicit, declare the hypothesized causal mechanism, control for the missing confounders, and justify their belief that none of the chosen explanatory variables is a collider.

If FF93, FF15, and C97 had proposed a predictive model, producing such biased estimates of the factor coefficients would not be problematic, because the prediction might still lead to a profitable investment strategy. However, as explained in

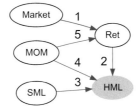

Figure 23 Example of a causal graph under which the findings in FF93, FF15, and C97 are biased

Section 6.1, the purpose of a factor model (such as FF93, FF15, and C97) is to build portfolios exposed to a particular risk characteristic presumably rewarded by the market. This is the reason value factor funds typically create a portfolio by ranking stocks in terms of their book-to-market ratio, not the model's residuals.

To summarize, the findings in FF93, FF15, and C97 are likely type-A spurious, due to *p*-hacking, or type-B spurious, due to under-controlling of confounders, over-controlling of mediators, specification-searching, and missing mediation analysis. This is not a criticism of these three papers relative to the rest of the factor investing literature. On the contrary, with all their flaws, these three papers are as good as any other associational financial econometric study, and continue to be deeply influential. Other papers in this field share the same or similar methodological errors that make their promoted factors likely spurious.

8 Conclusions

A scientific theory is a falsifiable statement of the form "X causes Y through mechanism M." Observed associations amount to phenomenological evidence, but do not rise to the status of scientific knowledge, for three reasons: (i) the observed association can be type-A spurious, due to p-hacking or backtest overfitting; (ii) even if true, the association is not necessarily causal; and (iii) even if causal, the association does not propose a falsifiable mechanism M by which X causes Y.

Scientific theories should matter to investors for at least three reasons: First, theories are a deterrent against type-A spuriosity, because they force scientists to justify their modelling choices, thus curtailing efforts to explain random variation (Section 6.4.1). A researcher who engages in p-hacking or backtest overfitting may build an *ad hoc* theory that explains an observed random variation. However, other researchers will use the theory to design an experiment where the original random variation is not observed (Section 3.3). Second, causality is a necessary condition for investment efficiency. Causal models allow investors to attribute risk and performance to the variables responsible for a phenomenon (Section 6.4.2). With proper attribution, investors can build a portfolio exposed only to rewarded risks, and aim for investment efficiency. In contrast, associational models misattribute risks and performance, thus preventing investors from building efficient portfolios. Third, causal models enable counterfactual reasoning, hence the stress-testing of investment portfolios in a coherent and forward-looking manner (see Rebonato 2010; Rebonato and Denev 2014; Denev 2015; Rodríguez-Domínguez 2023). In contrast, associational models cannot answer counterfactual questions, such as what would be the effect of Y on a not-yet-observed scenario X, thus exposing those relying on associations to black-swan events.

Despite the above, the majority of journal articles in the investment literature make associational claims and propose investment strategies designed to profit from those associations. For instance, authors may find that observation X often precedes the occurrence of event Y, determine that the correlation between X and Y is statistically significant, and propose a trading rule that presumably monetizes such correlation. A caveat of this reasoning is that the probabilistic statement "X often precedes Y" provides no evidence that Y is a function of X, thus the relationship between X and Y may be coincidental or unreliable. One possibility is that variables X and Y may appear to have been associated in the past by chance (type-A spuriosity), in which case the investment strategy will likely fail. Another possibility is that X and Y are associated even though Y is not a function of X (type-B spuriosity), for example due to a confounding variable Z which researchers have failed to control for, or due to a collider variable Z which researchers have mistaken for a confounder. These misspecification errors make it likely that the correlation between X and Y will change over time, and even reverse sign, exposing the investor to systematic losses.

The main conclusion of this Element is that, in its current formulation, factor investing has failed to achieve its objectives. Academically, it is a data-mining exercise that has yielded countless type-A and type-B spurious findings. Commercially, it is falsely promoted as a scientific product, and it has failed to deliver statistically significant returns, against the profit expectations generated by its promoters.

To find the path forward, factor researchers must first understand how they ended up with a black-box. Part of the answer is the strong grip that commercial interests hold on financial academia. Financial academics interested in starting over on the more solid foundations of causal factor investing should pursue collaborations with the research arms of noncommercial asset managers, such as sovereign wealth managers and endowments.

8.1 Factor Investing Is a Black-Box

Virtually all journal articles in the factor investing literature deny or ignore the causal content of factor models. Authors do not identify the causal graph consistent with the observed sample, they justify their chosen model specification in associational terms (e.g., optimizing the coefficient of determination), and they rarely theorize a falsifiable causal mechanism able to explain their findings. Absent a causal theory, it is nearly impossible to falsify their claims thoroughly (Section 3). It could take decades to collect enough out-of-sample evidence to determine that the association is false, and in-sample evidence is highly susceptible to p-hacking and backtest overfitting. The outcome from a backtest or a factor model is yet another associational claim, prone to the same misunderstandings and spurious claims discussed in Sections 5 and 6. For example, the factor models and backtests of strategies based on FF93, FF15, and C97 do not prove that holding value stocks causes a portfolio to outperform the market, because that causal claim can only be tested by the methods described in Section 4. Even if it were true that holding value stocks causes a portfolio to outperform the market, neither a factor model nor a backtest tells us why.

Consider the large losses experienced by value funds between late 2017 and early 2022. Investors never received a straight answer to the question "why did value funds perform so poorly?" The reason is, in absence of a causal theory, nobody knows why value funds should have performed well in the first place, or what turned the sign of value's $\hat{\beta}$ (a hallmark of type-B spurious factors, see Section 6.4.2). Asset managers will not admit their confusion to clients, as that would invite large-scale redemptions. Answering the "why" question requires a falsifiable causal mechanism, which to this day remains unknown for value investments.

Due to the omission of causal mechanisms (Section 6.2), factor investment strategies are promoted like associational investment strategies, through inductive arguments. For example, a researcher may find that value and momentum strategies have been profitable for many years (enumerative induction) or in many different geographies (variative induction). This associational finding generates the expectation that, whatever the unknown cause of value and momentum, and whatever the mechanism responsible for their profitability, history will continue to repeat itself, even though there is no scientific-deductive basis for such belief. Ironically, commercial asset managers routinely require investors to accept disclaimers such as "past performance is not indicative of future results," in direct contradiction with the inductive claims that authors promote and managers sell to customers.

Answering the "why" question is of particular importance for institutional investors, such as pension funds, sovereign wealth funds, endowments, and insurance companies. These investors manage funds for the benefit of the general public, and have a limited appetite for gambling. Factor investing may be an appropriate strategy for a high-net-worth individual, who can afford losing a large portion of his fortune. However, a salaried worker who has saved for 50 years and depends on those savings to retire should not be induced to wager his future wellbeing on investment strategies that, even if apparently profitable, are black-boxes. As long as asset managers remain unable to answer the "why" question, they should refrain from promoting to the general public factor investing products as scientific, and institutional investors should question whether factor investing products are investment grade.

8.2 The Economic Incentives for Associational Studies

In 2019, J.P. Morgan estimated that over USD 2.5 trillion (more than 20 percent of the US equity market capitalization) was managed by quant-style funds (Berman 2019). BlackRock estimates that the factor investing industry managed USD 1.9 trillion in 2017, and it projects that amount will grow to USD 3.4 trillion by 2022 (BlackRock 2017). This massive industry has been built on academic output, not on results for investors.

Harvey (2022) argues that economic incentives, instead of scientific considerations, may be driving the academic agenda. The financial industry funds associational studies, because they are cheaper and easier to produce than causal (scientific) studies, while they help achieve annual revenues in the tens of billions of US dollars. Unless asset owners demand change, the academic establishment will dismiss the need for causality, just as it continues to dismiss the existence of a reproducibility crisis caused by rampant *p*-hacking and backtest overfitting, in defiance of warnings issued by the American Statistical Association, the American Mathematical Society, and the Royal Statistical Society, among other scientific bodies.

8.3 The Dawn of Causal Factor Investing

Answering the "why" question is more than an academic pursuit. Causal factor theories would be highly beneficial to all types of investors, for several reasons: First, efficiency: causal models attribute risk and performance correctly. With proper risk and performance attribution, researchers can build portfolios that concentrate exposure on rewarded risks and hedge unrewarded risks. Second, interpretability: every institutional investor owes it to its beneficial owners to explain why they may have to delay their plans (e.g., retirement). Third, transparency: a causal graph makes explicit all the assumptions involved in a theorized mechanism. Investment strategies based on causal theories are not black-boxes. Fourth, reproducibility: a causal explanation reduces the chances of (i) random variation (type-A spuriosity), by confining the search space to plausible theories, and (ii) noncausal association (type-B spuriosity), by providing some assurances that the phenomenon will continue to occur as long as the mechanism remains. Fifth, adaptability: the profitability of investment strategies founded on associational relations relies on the stability of the joint distribution's parameters, which in turn depends on the stability of the entire causal graph (variable levels and parameters). In contrast, investment strategies based on causal relations are resilient to changes that do not involve the parameters in the causal path (see Section 6.4.2.1). This makes causal investment strategies more reliable than associational investment strategies. Sixth, extrapolation: only an investment strategy supported by a causal theory is equipped to survive and profit from black-swan events, by monitoring the conditions that trigger them (e.g., liquidity strategies based on the PIN theory performed well during the 2010 flash crash). Seventh, surveillance: the validity of a causal mechanism can be assessed in more direct and immediate ways than estimating the probability of a structural break in performance. This attribute is of critical importance in a complex dynamic system like finance: (i) an investor in a causal factor investing strategy may be able to divest when the causal mechanism weakens, before losses compound to the point that a statistical test detects a structural break; (ii) causal mechanisms enable factor timing, dynamic bet sizing, and tactical asset allocation. Eighth, improvability: causal theories can be refined, as a researcher learns more about the mechanism responsible for the observations. The fate of investment strategies based on causal theories is not unavoidable decay toward zero performance. These are all attributes that make an investment strategy appealing and trustworthy, and that current factor investments lack.

Financial economists' adoption of causal inference methods has the potential to transform investing into a truly scientific discipline. Economists are best positioned to inject, make explicit, and argue the extra-statistical information that complements and enriches the work of statisticians. Financial economists interested in causal research would do well in partnering with noncommercial asset managers, such as sovereign wealth funds and endowments. These institutional investors are not conflicted by commercial interests, and their objectives are aligned with their beneficial owners.

The new discipline of "causal factor investing" will be characterized by the adaptation and adoption of tools from causal discovery and do-calculus to the study of the risk characteristics that are responsible for differences in asset returns. Every year, new alternative datasets become available at an increasing rate, allowing researchers to conduct natural experiments and other types of causal inference that were not possible in the twentieth century. Causal factor investing will serve a social purpose beyond the reach of (associational) factor investing: help asset managers fulfill their fiduciary duties with the transparency and confidence that only the scientific method can deliver. To achieve this noble goal, the dawn of scientific investing, the factor investing community must first wake up from its associational slumber.

Appendix

A.1 Proof of Proposition in Section 6.4.2.1

Consider a data-generating process with equations:

$$X := Z\delta + v \tag{43}$$

$$Y := X\beta + Z\gamma + u \tag{44}$$

where $\gamma \neq 0$, $\delta \neq 0$, and variables (u, v, Z) are independent and identically distributed as a standard Normal, $(u, v, Z) \sim N[0, I]$. The causal graph for this process is displayed in Figure 10 (bottom). The process is unknown to observers, who attempt to estimate the causal effect of X on Y by fitting the equation $Y = X\beta + \varepsilon$ on a sample produced by the process. Then, the expression $E[\hat{\beta}|X]$ is,

$$E[\hat{\beta}|X] = (X'X)^{-1}X'E[Y|X]. \tag{45}$$

Replacing Y, we obtain

$$E[\hat{\beta}|X] = (X'X)^{-1}X'E[X\beta + Z\gamma + u|X]. \tag{46}$$

Since the expected value is conditioned by X, we replace Z to obtain

$$E[\hat{\beta}|X] = (X'X)^{-1}X'E[X\beta + \gamma\delta^{-1}(X - v) + u|X] =$$

$$(X'X)^{-1}X'\left(X\beta + \gamma\delta^{-1}X - \gamma\delta^{-1}E[v|X] + E[u|X]\right). \tag{47}$$

Knowledge of X does not convey information on u, hence $E[u|X] = 0$, however knowledge of X conveys information on v, since $X := Z\delta + v$. Accordingly, we can reduce the above expression to

$$E[\hat{\beta}|X] = \beta + \gamma\delta^{-1}(1 - (X'X)^{-1}X'E[v|X]). \tag{48}$$

This leaves us with an expression $E[v|X]$ that we would like to simplify. Note that variables (v, X) follow a Gaussian distribution with known mean and variance,

$$\begin{bmatrix} v \\ X \end{bmatrix} \sim N\left[\begin{pmatrix} 0 \\ 0 \end{pmatrix}, \begin{pmatrix} 1 & 1 \\ 1 & 1 + \delta^2 \end{pmatrix}\right] \tag{49}$$

$$v|X = x \sim N\mu, \Sigma). \tag{50}$$

We can compute $E[v|X]$ explicitly, using the formulas for the conditional Gaussian distribution (Eaton 1983, pp. 116–117),[39]

$$\mu = \mu_1 + \Sigma_{1,2}\Sigma_{2,2}^{-1}(x - \mu_2) =$$

$$0 + 1\left(1 + \delta^2\right)^{-1}(x - 0) =$$

$$\frac{x}{1 + \delta^2}. \tag{51}$$

For completeness, we can derive the variance Σ as

$$\Sigma = \Sigma_{1,1} - \Sigma_{1,2}\Sigma_{2,2}^{-1}\Sigma_{2,1} =$$

$$1 - 1\frac{1}{1 + \delta^2}1 =$$

$$\frac{\delta^2}{\delta^2 + 1}. \tag{52}$$

Using the above results, the expression of $E[\hat{\beta}|X]$ reduces to,

$$E[\hat{\beta}|X] = \beta + \gamma\delta\left(1 + \delta^2\right)^{-1}. \tag{53}$$

This completes the proof.

A.2 Proof of Proposition in Section 7.2

Consider the data-generating process with equations:

$$X_t := \epsilon_t \tag{54}$$

$$Y_t := \zeta_t \tag{55}$$

$$Z_t := X_t + Y_t + \xi_t \tag{56}$$

where $(\xi_t, \epsilon_t, \zeta_t)$ are three independent random variables that follow a standard Normal distribution, $(\xi_t, \epsilon_t, \zeta_t) \sim N[0, I]$. The random variable (X, Y, Z) is still Gaussian,

$$\begin{pmatrix} X \\ Y \\ Z \end{pmatrix} \sim N\left[\begin{pmatrix} 0 \\ 0 \\ 0 \end{pmatrix}, \begin{pmatrix} 1 & 0 & 1 \\ 0 & 1 & 1 \\ 1 & 1 & 3 \end{pmatrix}\right] = N\left[\begin{pmatrix} \mu_1 \\ \mu_2 \end{pmatrix}, \begin{pmatrix} \Sigma_{1,1} & \Sigma_{1,2} \\ \Sigma_{2,1} & \Sigma_{2,2} \end{pmatrix}\right]. \tag{57}$$

The conditional distribution has the form

---

[39] Special thanks to Vincent Zoonekynd for making this observation.

$$\begin{pmatrix} X \\ Y \end{pmatrix} \Big| Z = z \sim N[\mu, \Sigma] \tag{58}$$

where the parameters can be derived using the formulas for the conditional Gaussian distribution (Eaton 1983, pp. 116–117),

$$\mu = \mu_1 + \Sigma_{1,2}\Sigma_{2,2}^{-1}(z - \mu_2) =$$

$$\begin{pmatrix} 0 \\ 0 \end{pmatrix} + \begin{pmatrix} 1 \\ 1 \end{pmatrix} 3^{-1}z =$$

$$\begin{pmatrix} z/3 \\ z/3 \end{pmatrix} \tag{59}$$

$$\Sigma = \Sigma_{1,1} - \Sigma_{1,2}\Sigma_{2,2}^{-1}\Sigma_{2,1} =$$

$$\begin{pmatrix} 1 & 0 \\ 0 & 1 \end{pmatrix} - \begin{pmatrix} 1 \\ 1 \end{pmatrix} 3^{-1} (1 \quad 1) = \begin{pmatrix} 2/3 & -1/3 \\ -1/3 & 2/3 \end{pmatrix}. \tag{60}$$

Then, the covariance between X and Y conditional on Z is

$$Cov[X, Y|Z] = -\frac{1}{3}. \tag{61}$$

This completes the proof.

B.1 Code for Experiment in Section 7.1

Snippet 1 lists the Python 3 code used to produce the results of the Monte Carlo experiment that simulates a fork.

SNIPPET 1 FALSE POSITIVE DUE TO A CONFOUNDER

```python
import numpy as np, statsmodels.api as sm1
# Set data-generating process
np.random.seed(0)
z=np.random.normal(size=5000) # observable confounder
x=z+np.random.normal(size=z.shape[0]) # false cause
y=z+np.random.normal(size=z.shape[0]) # false effect
# Correct estimate of X->Y
X=np.column_stack((x,z))
ols1=sm1.OLS(y,sm1.add_constant(X)).fit()
print(ols1.summary(xname=['const','X','Z'],yname='Y')) # true negative
# Incorrect estimate of X->Y
ols0=sm1.OLS(y,sm1.add_constant(x)).fit()
print(ols0.summary(xname=['const','X'],yname='Y')) # false positive
```

B.2 Code for Experiment in Section 7.2

Snippet 2 lists the Python 3 code used to produce the results of the Monte Carlo experiment that simulates an immorality.

SNIPPET 2 FALSE POSITIVE DUE TO A COLLIDER

```
import numpy as np, statsmodels.api as sm1
# Set data-generating process
np.random.seed(0)
x=np.random.normal(size=5000) # false cause
y=np.random.normal(size=x.shape[0]) # false effect
z=x+y+np.random.normal(size=x.shape[0]) # collider
# Correct estimate of X->Y
ols0=sm1.OLS(y,sm1.add_constant(x)).fit()
print(ols0.summary(xname=['const','X'],yname='Y')) # true negative
# Incorrect estimate of X->Y
X=np.column_stack((x,z))
ols1=sm1.OLS(y,sm1.add_constant(X)).fit()
print(ols1.summary(xname=['const','X','Z'],yname='Y')) # false positive
```

B.3 Code for Experiment in Section 7.3

Snippet 3 lists the Python 3 code used to produce the results of the Monte Carlo experiment that simulates a chain.

SNIPPET 3 FALSE POSITIVE DUE TO A CONFOUNDED MEDIATOR

```
import numpy as np, statsmodels.api as sm1
# Set data-generating process
np.random.seed(0)
x=np.random.normal(size=5000) # cause
w=np.random.normal(size=x.shape[0]) # confounder
z=x+w+np.random.normal(size=x.shape[0]) # mediator
y=z+w+np.random.normal(size=x.shape[0]) # effect
# Correct estimate of X->Y
ols1=sm1.OLS(y,sm1.add_constant(x)).fit()
print(ols1.summary(xname=['const','X'],yname='Y')) # true positive
# Incorrect estimate of X->Y
X=np.column_stack((x,z))
ols1=sm1.OLS(y,sm1.add_constant(X)).fit()
print(ols1.summary(xname=['const','X','Z'],yname='Y')) # false positive
```

References

Abadie, A. (2021): "Using Synthetic Controls: Feasibility, Data Requirements, and Methodological Aspects." *Journal of Economic Literature*, Vol. 59, No. 2, pp. 391–425.

Abadie, A. and M. Cattaneo (2018): "Econometric Methods for Program Evaluation." *Annual Review of Economics*, Vol. 10, pp. 465–503.

Anderson, R. (2011): "Time-Varying Risk Premia." *Journal of Mathematical Economics*, Vol. 47, No. 3, pp. 253–259.

Angrist, J. and J. Pischke (2008): *Mostly Harmless Econometrics: An Empiricist's Companion*. Princeton University Press, 1st ed.

Angrist, J. and J. Pischke (2010): "The Credibility Revolution in Empirical Economics: How Better Research Design Is Taking the Con out of Econometrics." *National Bureau of Economic Research*, Working Paper 15794. www.nber.org/papers/w15794.

Ashenfelter, O. and D. Card (1986): "Why Have Unemployment Rates in Canada and the United States Diverged?" *Economica*, Vol. 53, No. 210, pp. S171–S195.

Athey, S. and G. Imbens (2019): "Machine Learning Methods That Economists Should Know about." *Annual Review of Economics*, Vol. 11, pp. 685–725.

Baba, K., R. Shibata, and M. Sibuya (2004): "Partial Correlation and Conditional Correlation as Measures of Conditional Independence." *Australian and New Zealand Journal of Statistics*, Vol. 46, No. 4, pp. 657–664.

Bailey, D., J. Borwein, M. López de Prado, and J. Zhu (2014): "Pseudo-Mathematics and Financial Charlatanism: The Effects of Backtest Overfitting on Out-of-Sample Performance." *Notices of the American Mathematical Society*, Vol. 61, No. 5, pp. 458–471.

Bailey, D. and M. López de Prado (2012): "The Sharpe Ratio Efficient Frontier." *Journal of Risk*, Vol. 15, No. 2, pp. 3–44.

Bailey, D. and M. López de Prado (2014): "The Deflated Sharpe Ratio: Correcting for Selection Bias, Backtest Overfitting and Non-Normality." *Journal of Portfolio Management*, Vol. 40, No. 5, pp. 94–107.

Bailey, D. and M. López de Prado (2021): "How 'Backtest Overfitting' in Finance Leads to False Discoveries." *Significance (Royal Statistical Society)*, Vol. 18, No. 6, pp. 22–25.

Baker, M. and J. Wurgler (2007): "Investor Sentiment in the Stock Market." *Journal of Economic Perspectives*, Vol. 21, No. 2, pp. 129–152.

Balsubramani, A. and A. Ramdas (2016): "Sequential Nonparametric Testing with the Law of the Iterated Logarithm." *ArXiv*, Working Paper. https://arxiv.org/pdf/1506.03486.pdf.

Barroso, P. and P. Santa-Clara (2015): "Momentum Has Its Moments." *Journal of Financial Economics*, Vol. 116, No. 1, pp. 111–120.

Benjamini, Y. and Y. Hochberg (1995): "Controlling the False Discovery Rate: A Practical and Powerful Approach to Multiple Testing." *Journal of the Royal Statistical Society, Series B*, Vol. 57, No. 1, pp. 125–133.

Berk, J., R. Green, and V. Naik (1999): "Optimal Investment, Growth Options, and Security Returns." *Journal of Finance*, Vol. 54, pp. 1153–1607.

Berkson, J. (1946): "Limitations of the Application of Fourfold Table Analysis to Hospital Data." *Biometrics Bulletin*, Vol. 2, No. 3, pp. 47–53.

BlackRock 2017. www.hvst.com/posts/factors-making-waves-andrews-angle-X7QTZkL6.

BlackRock (2022): "What Is Factor Investing?" www.blackrock.com/us/individual/investment-ideas/what-is-factor-investing.

Bloomberg (2021): "Bloomberg GSAM US Equity Multi Factor Index." *Bloomberg Professional Services – Indices*. Available through the Bloomberg Terminal. https://assets.bbhub.io/professional/sites/10/Bloomberg-GSAM-US-Equity-Multi-Factor-Index-Fact-Sheet.pdf

Bronzoni, R. and E. Iachini (2014): "Are Incentives for R&D Effective? Evidence from a Regression Discontinuity Approach." *American Economic Journal: Economic Policy*, Vol. 6, No. 4, pp. 100–134.

Carhart, M. (1997): "On Persistence in Mutual Fund Performance." *Journal of Finance*, Vol. 52, No. 1, pp. 57–82.

Chatfield, C. (1995): "Model Uncertainty, Data Mining and Statistical Inference." *Journal of the Royal Statistical Society. Series A*, Vol. 158, No. 3, pp. 419–466.

Chen, B. and J. Pearl (2013): "Regression and Causation: A Critical Examination of Six Econometrics Textbooks." *Real-World Economics Review*, No. 65, pp. 2–20. http://www.paecon.net/PAEReview/issue65/ChenPearl65.pdf.

Chickering, D. (2003): "Optimal Structure Identification with Greedy Search." *Journal of Machine Learning Research*, Vol. 3, pp. 507–554.

Cochrane, J. (2005): *Asset Pricing*. Princeton University Press, 1st ed.

Cochrane, J. (2011): "Presidential Address: Discount Rates." *Journal of Finance*, Vol. 66, No. 4, pp. 1047–1108.

Cong, L., K. Tang, J. Wang, and Y. Zhang (2021): "AlphaPortfolio: Direct Construction through Deep Reinforcement Learning and Interpretable AI." *SSRN*, Working Paper. https://ssrn.com/abstract=3554486.

Das, S. and M. Chen (2007): "Yahoo! For Amazon: Sentiment Extraction from Small Talk on the Web." *Management Science*, Vol. 53, No. 9, pp. 1375–1388.

De Miguel, V., L. Garlappi, and R. Uppal (2009): "Optimal versus Naive Diversification: How Inefficient Is the 1/N Portfolio Strategy?" *Review of Financial Studies*, Vol. 22, No. 5, pp. 1915–1953.

Denev, A. (2015): *Probabilistic Graphical Models: A New Way of Thinking in Financial Modelling*. Risk Books, 1st ed.

Dickson, M. and D. Baird (2011): "Significance Testing." In *Philosophy of Statistics*, pp. 199–232, edited by P. Bandyopadhyay and M. Forster. Elsevier, 1st ed.

Diebold, F. (2007): *Elements of Forecasting*. Thomson South-Western, 4th ed.

Dryden, J. (1697): *The Works of Virgil Containing His Pastorals, Georgics and Aeneis*. https://quod.lib.umich.edu/e/eebo/A65112.0001.001/1:18.2? rgn=div2;view=fulltext.

Dunning, T. (2012): *Natural Experiments in the Social Sciences: A Design-Based Approach*. Cambridge University Press, 1st ed.

Easley, D., N. Kiefer, M. O'Hara, and J. Paperman (1996): "Liquidity, Information, and Infrequently Traded Stocks." *Journal of Finance*, Vol. 51, No. 4, pp. 1405–1436.

Easley, D., M. López de Prado, and M. O'Hara (2010): "Measuring Flow Toxicity in a High-Frequency World." SSRN Working Paper. http://ssrn .com/abstract=1695596.

Easley, D., M. López de Prado, and M. O'Hara (2012): "Flow Toxicity and Liquidity in a High-Frequency World." *Review of Financial Studies*, Vol. 25, No. 5, pp. 1457–1493.

Easley, D., M. López de Prado, and M. O'Hara (2016): "Discerning Information from Trade Data." *Journal of Financial Economics*, Vol. 120, No. 2, pp. 269–285.

Eaton, M. (1983): *Multivariate Statistics: A Vector Space Approach*. Wiley, 1st ed.

Efron, B. and T. Hastie (2021): *Computer Age Statistical Inference: Algorithms, Evidence, and Data Science*. Cambridge University Press, 1st ed. https:// hastie.su.domains/CASI_files/PDF/casi.pdf.

Evans, M. (1994): "Expected Returns, Time-Varying Risk, and Risk Premia." *Journal of Finance*, Vol. 49, No. 2, pp. 655–679.

Fabozzi, F. and M. López de Prado (2018): "Being Honest in Backtest Reporting: A Template for Disclosing Multiple Tests." *Journal of Portfolio Management*, Vol. 45, No. 1, pp. 141–147.

Fama, E. (1970): "Efficient Capital Markets: A Review of Theory and Empirical Work." *Journal of Finance*, Vol. 25, No. 2, pp. 383–417.

Fama, E. and K. French (1993): "Common Risk Factors in the Returns on Stocks and Bonds." *Journal of Financial Economics*, Vol. 33, No. 1, pp. 3–56.

Fama, E. and K. French (1996): "Multifactor Explanations of Asset Pricing Anomalies." *Journal of Finance*, Vol. 51, No. 1, pp. 55–84.

Fama, E. and K. French (2015): "A Five-Factor Asset Pricing Model." *Journal of Financial Economics*, Vol. 116, No. 1, pp. 1–22.

Fama, E. and J. MacBeth (1973): "Risk Return and Equilibrium: Empirical Tests." *Journal of Political Economy*, Vol. 71, pp. 607–636.

Ferson, W. (2019): *Empirical Asset Pricing: Models and Methods*. MIT Press, 1st ed.

Fisher, R. (1971): *The Design of Experiments*. Macmillan, 9th ed.

Flammer, C. (2015): "Corporate Social Responsibility and the Allocation of Procurement Contracts: Evidence from a Natural Experiment." Working Paper, Boston University. https://corporate-sustainability.org/wp-content/uploads/Corporate-Social-Responsibility.pdf.

Gelman, A. and C. Rohilla-Shalizi (2013): "Philosophy and the Practice of Bayesian Statistics." *British Journal of Mathematical and Statistical Psychology*, Vol. 66, pp. 8–38.

Gensler, H. (2010): *Introduction to Logic*. Routledge, 2nd ed.

Glymour, C., K. Zhang, and P. Spirtes (2019): "Review of Causal Discovery Methods Based on Graphical Models." *Frontiers in Genetics*, Vol. 10, p. 524. pp. 1–15, www.frontiersin.org/articles/10.3389/fgene.2019.00524/full.

Gomes, J., L. Kogan, and L. Zhang (2003): "Equilibrium Cross Section of Returns." *Journal of Political Economy*, Vol. 111, pp. 693–732.

Granger, C. (1969): "Investigating Causal Relations by Econometric Models and Cross-Spectral Methods." *Econometrica*, Vol. 37, No. 3, pp. 424–438.

Granger, C. and P. Newbold (1974): "Spurious Regressions in Econometrics." *Journal of Econometrics*, Vol. 2, No. 2, pp. 111–120.

Granger, C. (1980): "Testing for Causality: A Personal Viewpoint." *Journal of Economic Dynamics and Control*, Vol. 2, pp. 329–352.

Granger, C., N. Hyung, and Y. Jeon (2001): "Spurious Regressions with Stationary Series." *Applied Economics*, Vol. 33, No. 7, pp. 899–904.

Greene, W. (2012): *Econometric Analysis*. Pearson Education, 7th ed.

Haavelmo, T. (1944): "The probability approach in econometrics." *Econometrica*, Vol. 12, Supplement (July, 1944), pp. 1–115.

Hamilton, J. (1994): *Time Series Analysis*. Princeton, 1st ed.

Harvey, C., Y. Liu, and H. Zhu (2016): ". . . and the Cross-Section of Expected Returns." *Review of Financial Studies*, Vol. 29, No. 1, pp. 5–68.

Harvey, C. (2017): "Presidential Address: The Scientific Outlook in Financial Economics." *Journal of Finance*, Vol. 72, No. 4, pp. 1399–1440.

Harvey, C. (2022): "The Pitfalls of Asset Management Research." *Journal of Systematic Investment*, Vol. 2, No. 1, pp. 1–9. https://papers.ssrn.com/sol3/papers.cfm?abstract_id=4078138.

Hassani, H., X. Huang, and M. Ghodsi (2018): "Big Data and Causality." *Annals of Data Science*, Vol. 5, pp. 133–156.

Heilbron, J. (ed.) (2003): "Preface." In *The Oxford Companion to the History of Modern Science*. Oxford University Press, pp. vii–x.

Hernán, M. and J. Robins (2020): *Causal Inference: What If*. CRC Press, 1st ed.

Hill, R., W. Griffiths, and G. Lim (2011): *Principles of Econometrics*. John Wiley, 4th ed.

Hochberg, Y. (1988): "A Sharper Bonferroni Procedure for Multiple Tests of Significance." *Biometrika*, Vol. 75, pp. 800–802.

Hoyer, P., D. Janzing, J. Mooji, J. Peters, and B. Schölkopf (2009): "Nonlinear Causal Discovery with Additive Noise Models." In *Advances in Neural Information Processing Systems*, edited by Michael I. Jordan, Yann LeCun, and Sara A. Solla. Vol. 21. https://mitpress.mit.edu/9780262561457/advances-in-neural-information-processing-systems/.

Imai, K. (2013): "Statistical Hypothesis Tests." Course Materials, Department of Politics, Princeton University. https://imai.fas.harvard.edu/teaching/files/tests.pdf.

Imbens, G. and T. Lemieux (2008): "Regression Discontinuity Designs: A Guide to Practice." *Journal of Econometrics*, Vol. 142, No. 2, pp. 615–635.

Imbens, G. and J. Wooldridge (2009): "Recent Developments in the Econometrics of Program Evaluation." *Journal of Econometric Literature*, Vol. 47, pp. 5–86.

Isichenko, M. (2021): *Quantitative Portfolio Management: The Art and Science of Statistical Arbitrage*. Wiley, 1st ed.

Johnson, T. (2002): "Rational Momentum Effects." *Journal of Finance*, Vol. 57, pp. 585–608.

Jones, B. and M. Kenward (2003): *Design and Analysis of Cross-Over Trials*. London: Chapman & Hall/CRC, 2nd ed.

Kalnins, A. (2022): "When Does Multicollinearity Bias Coefficients and Cause Type 1 Errors? A Reconciliation of Lindner, Puck, and Verbeke (2020) with Kalnins (2018)." *Journal of International Business Studies*, Vol. 53, pp. 1536–1548.

Katayama, D. and K. Tsuda (2020): "A Method of Using News Sentiment for Stock Investment Strategy." *Procedia Computer Science*, Vol. 176, pp. 1971–1980.

Kennedy, P. (2008): *A Guide to Econometrics*. MIT Press, 6th ed.

Kohavi, R., D. Tang, Y. Xu, L. Hemkens, and J. Ioannidis (2020): "Online Randomized Controlled Experiments at Scale: Lessons and Extensions to

Medicine." *Trials*, Vol. 21 Article 150, pp. 1–9. https://trialsjournal.biomed central.com/articles/10.1186/s13063-020-4084-y.

Koller, D. and N. Friedman (2009): *Probabilistic Graphical Models: Principles and Techniques*. Adaptive Computation and Machine Learning. MIT Press, 1st ed.

Lakatos, I. (1978): *The Methodology of Scientific Research Programmes*. Philosophical Papers, Vol. 1. Cambridge University Press, 1st ed.

Laudy O., A. Denev, and A. Ginsberg (2022): "Building Probabilistic Causal Models Using Collective Intelligence." *The Journal of Financial Data Science*, Vol. 4, No. 2, pp. 83–109.

Lazear, E. (2000): "Economic Imperialism." *The Quarterly Journal of Economics*, Vol. 115, No. 1, pp. 99–146.

Leamer, E. (1983): "Let's Take the Con Out of Econometrics." *American Economic Review*, Vol. 73, No. 1, pp. 31–43.

Li, D. and L. Zhang (2010): "Does q-Theory with Investment Frictions Explain Anomalies in the Cross-Section of Returns?" *Journal of Financial Economics*, Vol. 98, pp. 297–314.

Li, E., D. Livdan, and L. Zhang (2009): "Anomalies." *Review of Financial Studies*, Vol. 22, pp. 4301–4334.

Lipton, A. (2016): "Macroeconomic Theories: Not Even Wrong." *Risk*, August 22. www.risk.net/cutting-edge/views/2468446/macroeconomic-the ories-not-even-wrong.

Liu, L., T. Whited, and L. Zhang (2009): "Investment-Based Expected Stock Returns." *Journal of Political Economy*, Vol. 117, pp. 1105–1139.

Liu, L. and L. Zhang (2008): "Momentum Profits, Factor Pricing, and Macroeconomic Risk." *Review of Financial Studies*, Vol. 21, pp. 2417–2448.

López de Prado, M. (2017): "Finance as an Industrial Science." *Journal of Portfolio Management*, Vol. 43, No. 4, pp. 5–9.

López de Prado, M. (2018): *Advances in Financial Machine Learning*. Wiley, 1st ed.

López de Prado, M. (2019): "A Data Science Solution to the Multiple-Testing Crisis in Financial Research." *Journal of Financial Data Science*, Vol. 1, No. 1, pp. 99–110.

López de Prado, M. (2020): *Machine Learning for Asset Managers*. Cambridge University Press, 1st ed.

López de Prado, M. (2022a): "Machine Learning for Econometricians: A ReadMe Manual." *Journal of Financial Data Science*, Vol. 4, No. 3, pp. 1–21.

López de Prado, M. (2022b): "Type I and Type II Errors of the Sharpe Ratio under Multiple Testing." *Journal of Portfolio Management*, Vol. 49, No. 1, pp. 39–46.

López de Prado, M. and D. Bailey (2020): "The False Strategy Theorem: A Financial Application of Experimental Mathematics." *American Mathematical Monthly*, Vol. 128, No. 9, pp. 825–831.

López de Prado, M. and M. Lewis (2019): "Detection of False Investment Strategies Using Unsupervised Learning Methods." *Quantitative Finance*, Vol. 19, No. 9, pp. 1555–1565.

Malenko, N. and Y. Shen (2016): "The Role of Proxy Advisory Firms: Evidence from a Regression-Discontinuity Design." *Review of Financial Studies*, Vol. 29, No. 12, pp. 3394–3427.

Mullainathan, S. and J. Spiess (2017): "Machine Learning: An Applied Econometric Approach." *Journal of Economic Perspectives*, Vol. 31, No. 2, pp. 87–106.

Neal, B. (2020): *Introduction to Causal Inference: From a Machine Learning Perspective*. Course Lecture Notes (December 17, 2020). www.bradyneal .com/causal-inference-course.

Neuberger Berman (2019): "Inside the Quant Investing Trend." *Quarterly Views*. www.nb.com/documents/public/en-us/Messinger_Client_Letter_2Q19.pdf.

Pearl, J. (1995): "Causal Diagrams for Empirical Research." *Biometrika*, Vol. 82, pp. 669–710.

Pearl, J. (2009): *Causality: Models, Reasoning and Inference*. Cambridge, 2nd ed.

Pearl, J. (2015): "Trygve Haavelmo and the Emergence of Causal Calculus." *Econometric Theory*, Vol. 31, pp. 152–179.

Pearl, J., M. Glymour, and N. Jewell (2016): *Causal Inference in Statistics: A Primer*. Wiley, 1st ed.

Pearl, J. and D. MacKenzie (2018): *The Book of Why*. Basic Books, 1st ed.

Peierls, R. (1992): "Where Pauli Made His 'Wrong' Remark." *Physics Today*, Vol. 45, No. 12, p. 112.

Perezgonzalez, J. (2017): "Commentary: The Need for Bayesian Hypothesis Testing in Psychological Science." *Frontiers of Psychology*, Vol. 8, Article 1434 pp. 1–3.

Peters, L., D. Janzing, and B. Scholkopf (2017): *Elements of Causal Inference: Foundations and Learning Algorithms*. MIT Press, 1st ed.

Pogosian, L., M. Raveri, K. Koyama et al. (2022): "Imprints of Cosmological Tensions in Reconstructed Gravity." *Nature Astronomy*, Vol. 6, pp. 1484–1490. Forthcoming. https://doi.org/10.1038/s41550-022-01808-7.

Popper, K. (1963): *Conjectures and Refutations*. Routledge and Kegan Paul, 1st ed.

Popper, K. (1994a): "Falsifizierbarkeit, zwei Bedeutungen von." In *Handlexikon zur Wissenschaftstheorie*, pp. 82–86, edited by H. Seiffert and G. Radnitzky. Ehrenwirth GmbH Verlag, 2nd ed.

Popper, K. (1994b): *The Myth of the Framework. In Defense of Science and Rationality.* Routledge, 1st ed.

Rad, H., R. Low, and R. Faff (2016): "The Profitability of Pairs Trading Strategies: Distance, Cointegration and Copula Methods." *Quantitative Finance*, Vol. 16, No. 10, pp. 1541–1558.

Rao, C. (2000): *Understanding Chemistry.* Universities Press, 1st ed.

Rebonato, R. (2010): *Coherent Stress Testing.* Wiley, 1st ed.

Rebonato, R. and A. Denev (2014): *Portfolio Management under Stress: A Bayesian-Net Approach to Coherent Asset Allocation.* Cambridge University Press, 1st ed.

Reeves, C. and J. Brewer (1980): "Hypothesis Testing and Proof By Contradiction: An Analogy." *Teaching Statistics*, Vol. 2, No. 2, pp. 57–59.

Robins, J. (1986): "A New Approach to Causal Inference in Mortality Studies with a Sustained Exposure Period: Application to Control of a Healthy Worker Survivor Effect." *Mathematical Modelling*, Vol. 7, No. 9–12, pp. 1393–1512.

Rodríguez-Domínguez, A. (2023): "Portfolio Optimization Based on Neural Networks Sensitivities from Asset Dynamics Respect Common Drivers." *Machine Learning with Applications*, Vol. 11, pp. 1–17. https://arxiv.org/abs/2202.08921.

Romano, J. and M. Wolf (2005): "Stepwise Multiple Testing as Formalized Data Snooping." *Econometrica*, Vol. 73, No. 4, pp. 1237–1282.

Ruud, P. (2000): *An Introduction to Classical Econometric Theory.* Oxford University Press.

Sabra, A. (1989): *The Optics of Ibn al-Haytham. Books I-II-III: On Direct Vision.* The Warburg Institute, University of London, 1st ed.

Sagi, J. and M. Seasholes (2007): "Firm-Specific Attributes and the Cross-Section of Momentum." *Journal of Financial Economics*, Vol. 84, pp. 389–434.

Schipper, K. and R. Thompson (1981): "Common Stocks as Hedges against Shifts in the Consumption or Investment Opportunity Set." *Journal of Business*, Vol. 1, pp. 305–328.

Schuller, M., A. Haberl, and I. Zaichenkov (2021): "Causality Testing in Equity Markets." Working Paper. https://papers.ssrn.com/sol3/papers.cfm?abstract_id=3941647.

Shimizu, S., P. Hoyer, A. Hyvärinen, and A. Kerminen (2006): "A Linear Non-Gaussian Acyclic Model for Causal Discovery." *Journal of Machine Learning Research*, Vol. 7, pp. 2003–2030.

Shpitser, I. and J. Pearl (2006): "Identification of Joint Interventional Distributions in Recursive Semi-Markovian Causal Models." *Proceedings of the Twenty-First National Conference on Artificial Intelligence.* AAAI Press, pp. 1219–1226.

Spirtes, P., C. Glymour, and R. Scheines (2000): "Constructing Bayesian Networks Models of Gene Expression Networks from Microarray Data." *Proceedings of the Atlantic Symposium on Computational Biology* (North Carolina). https://kilthub.cmu.edu/articles/journal_contribution/Constructing_Bayesian_Network_Models_of_Gene_Expression_Networks_from_Microarray_Data/6491291.

Spirtes, P., C. Glymour, and R. Scheines (2001): *Causation, Prediction, and Search*. MIT Press, 2nd ed.

Thiele, R. (2005): "In Memoriam: Matthias Schramm, 1928–2005." *Historia Mathematica*, Vol. 32, pp. 271–274.

Toomer, G. (1964): "Review: Ibn al-Haythams Weg zur Physik by Matthias Schramm." *Isis*, Vol. 55, No. 4, pp. 463–465.

Vignero, L. and S. Wenmackers (2021): "Degrees of Riskiness, Falsifiability, and Truthlikeness." *Synthese*, Vol. 199, pp. 11729–11764. https://doi.org/10.1007/s11229-021-03310-5.

Vlastos, G. (1983): "The Socratic Elenchus." *Oxford Studies in Ancient Philosophy*. Oxford University Press, 1st ed.

Wasserstein, R. and N. Lazar (2016): "The ASA Statement on p-Values: Context, Process, and Purpose." *The American Statistician*, Vol. 70, No. 2, pp. 129–133.

Webster, K. and N. Westray (2022): "Getting More for Less: Better A/B Testing via Causal Regularization." Working Paper. https://ssrn.com/abstract_id=4160945.

White, H. (2000): "A Reality Check for Data Snooping." *Econometrica*, Vol. 68, No. 5, pp. 1097–1126.

Wieten, R., F. Bex, H. Prakken, and S. Renooij (2020): "Deductive and Abductive Reasoning with Causal and Evidential Information." In *Computational Modes of Arguments*, pp. 383–394, edited by H. Prakken, S. Bistarelli, F. Santini, and C. Taticchi. IOS Press, 1st ed. www.florisbex.com/papers/COMMA2020IGN.pdf.

Wilkinson, M. (2013): "Testing the Null Hypothesis: The Forgotten Legacy of Karl Popper?" *Journal of Sports Sciences*, Vol. 31, No. 9, pp. 919–920.

Wooldridge, J. (2009): *Should Instrumental Variables Be Used as Matching Variables?* Technical Report, Michigan State University. www.msu.edu/~ec/faculty/wooldridge/current%20research/treat1r6.pdf.

Zhang, K. and A. Hyvärinen (2009): "On the Identifiability of the Post-Nonlinear Causal Model." *Proceedings of the 25th Conference on Uncertainty in Artificial Intelligence*. https://arxiv.org/abs/1205.2599.

Zhang, L. (2005): "The Value Premium." *Journal of Finance*, Vol. 60, pp. 67–103.

Acknowledgments

The views expressed in this Element are the author's, and do not necessarily represent the opinions of the organizations he is affiliated with. Special thanks are due to Majed AlRomaithi, Alexander Lipton, Jean-Paul Villain, and Vincent Zoonekynd, for numerous comments and contributions. The Element has also benefited from conversations with more ADIA colleagues than I can cite here, as well as Victoria Averbukh (Cornell University), David H. Bailey (Berkeley Lab), David Easley (Cornell University), Frank Fabozzi (EDHEC), Campbell Harvey (Duke University), John Hull (University of Toronto), Alessia López de Prado Rehder (ETH Zurich), Maureen O'Hara (Cornell University), Emilio Porcu (Khalifa University), Riccardo Rebonato (EDHEC), Alessio Sancetta (Royal Holloway, University of London), Luis Seco (University of Toronto), Sasha Stoikov (Cornell University), Josef Teichmann (ETH Zurich), and Jorge Zubelli (Khalifa University).

I would like to express my gratitude to the members of ADIA Lab's Executive Board, for supporting the publication of this Element as Open Access: Abdulla AlKetbi (Chair), Fatima Almheiri (Vice-Chair), Khamis AlKhyeli, Humaid AlKaabi, Ahmed Almheiri, and Marwan AlRemeithi.

Finally, ADIA Lab's Advisory Board comprises esteemed colleagues who are a constant source of inspiration: Horst Simon (Director), Steven Chu (Stanford University), Jack Dongarra (University of Tennessee), Shafi Goldwasser (UC Berkeley), Miguel Hernán (Harvard), Edward Jung (Intellectual Ventures), Alexander Lipton (Hebrew University), and Alexander Pentland (MIT).

About the Author

Marcos López de Prado is Global Head of Quantitative Research and Development at the Abu Dhabi Investment Authority, a founding board member of ADIA Lab, and Professor of Practice at Cornell University's School of Engineering, where he teaches machine learning. In recognition of his work, Marcos has received various scientific and industry awards, including the National Award for Academic Excellence (1999) by the Kingdom of Spain, the Quant Researcher of the Year Award (2019) by The Journal of Portfolio Management, and the Buy-Side Quant of the Year Award (2021) by Risk.net. For more information, visit www.QuantResearch.org

About ADIA Lab

ADIA Lab is an independent institution engaged in basic and applied research in Data Science, Artificial Intelligence, Machine Learning, and High-Performance Computing, across all major fields of study. This includes exploring applications in areas such as climate change and energy transition, blockchain technology, financial inclusion and investing, decision making, automation, cybersecurity, health sciences, education, telecommunications, and space.

Based in Abu Dhabi, ADIA Lab is an independent, standalone entity supported by the Abu Dhabi Investment Authority (ADIA), a globally-diversified investment institution that invests funds on behalf of the Government of Abu Dhabi.

ADIA Lab has its own governance and operational structure, and is guided by an Advisory Board of global thought-leaders in data and computationally-intensive disciplines, including winners of the Nobel, Turing, Gödel, Rousseeuw, Gordon Bell, and other prizes.

Cambridge Elements ☰

Quantitative Finance

Riccardo Rebonato

EDHEC Business School

Editor Riccardo Rebonato is Professor of Finance at EDHEC Business School and holds the PIMCO Research Chair for the EDHEC Risk Institute. He has previously held academic positions at Imperial College, London, and Oxford University and has been Global Head of Fixed Income and FX Analytics at PIMCO, and Head of Research, Risk Management and Derivatives Trading at several major international banks. He has previously been on the Board of Directors for ISDA and GARP, and he is currently on the Board of the Nine Dot Prize. He is the author of several books and articles in finance and risk management, including *Bond Pricing and Yield Curve Modelling* (2017, Cambridge University Press).

About the Series

Cambridge *Elements in Quantitative Finance* aims for broad coverage of all major topics within the field. Written at a level appropriate for advanced undergraduate or graduate students and practitioners, *Elements* combines reports on original research covering an author's personal area of expertise, tutorials and masterclasses on emerging methodologies, and reviews of the most important literature.

Cambridge Elements ≡

Quantitative Finance

Printed in the United States
by Baker & Taylor Publisher Services